Distracted from Meaning

Distracted from Meaning

A Philosophy of Smartphones

Tiger C. Roholt

BLOOMSBURY ACADEMIC

LONDON • NEW YORK • OXFORD • NEW DELHI • SYDNEY

BLOOMSBURY ACADEMIC
Bloomsbury Publishing Plc
50 Bedford Square, London, WC1B 3DP, UK
1385 Broadway, New York, NY 10018, USA
29 Earlsfort Terrace, Dublin 2, Ireland

BLOOMSBURY, BLOOMSBURY ACADEMIC and the Diana logo are trademarks
of Bloomsbury Publishing Plc
First published in Great Britain 2023
Copyright © Tiger C. Roholt, 2023

For Jill Rosenberg

Contents

Acknowledgments

Portions of Chapters 2 and 6 draw on my "Being-with Smartphones," *Techné: Research in Philosophy and Technology* 25, no. 2 (2021). Chapter 5 draws on my "Performance, Technology, and the Good Life," in *The Oxford Handbook of the Phenomenology of Music*, edited by Jonathan De Souza, Benjamin Steege, and Jessica Wiskus (Oxford: Oxford University Press, forthcoming). I owe thanks to these reviewers and editors for their very helpful comments. I also want to thank Jane Vincent, the reviewers and editors at Bloomsbury Academic (especially Colleen Coalter), and Jill Rosenberg. Thank you to Kirk, Meghan, Jon, our students—and many other philosophy enthusiasts—who have made Montclair's *Philosophy for Lunch* into a weekly focal practice. Finally, I am grateful for the support of Dorothy, Les, and Shira Roholt, Henrietta and Henry Rosenberg, and Greta Roholt-Rosenberg.

1

Introduction

We are bringing smartphones into the areas of our lives where we engage with our friends, loved ones, and the projects that shape our identities. We are doing this without understanding how smartphones fit into these situations or what effects they might have. We need a better grasp of this relatively new, influential factor in our lives. Here, I take up a central aspect of this challenge; this book is an exploration of smartphone-distraction and its impact on meaningful activities, experiences, and projects.

We tend to be unaware that smartphones distract us from certain kinds of activities that add meaning to our lives.[1] Which kinds of activities? Consider two: smartphones can distract us from certain work we do to shape our self-identities (Chapter 6). In addition, smartphones can distract us from experiences that are not momentary but which we actively cultivate over many minutes or even hours (Chapter 3). We will see that both kinds of activities are related to the cultivation of meaning in life. Yet, when concerns about smartphone-distraction are raised (for example in social-science studies) activities and experiences like these are not considered.

There is another class of meaningful activities regarding which we *are* aware that smartphone-distraction is problematic, but even in these cases clarity is lacking. Consider our engagement with what Albert Borgmann calls focal practices, such as a dinner with friends or family, a hike, attending a football game with friends, or a small musical performance (Chapter 5).[2] Many of us recognize that smartphones may distract us during these kinds of activities. And many of us recognize that these activities are potentially meaningful in some sense. But regarding these cases, as well as the cases mentioned in the previous paragraph, more clarity is needed about what makes these activities meaningful. In addition, we need a better understanding of the operative mechanisms of smartphone-distraction, as well as this distraction's effects on such activities. Take these to be two perplexities already on the table: I want a clearer picture of meaningfulness, and, I want a clearer picture of the ways in which smartphones can interfere with the cultivation of this meaning. Throughout this book, I will be attempting to clarify both perplexities.

In order to clarify the ways in which smartphone-use might interfere with meaningful activities, we need an account of meaning in life. Moreover, this account cannot be too abstract; it must provide the detail that enables us to inspect concrete situations in which a person's smartphone-use may distract her from engaging effectively with an activity that is potentially meaningful.

We will find a portion of the experiential and behavioral detail needed by drawing upon John Dewey's writing on experience (Chapter 3). Dewey offers a rich account of experience through his notion of "*an* experience." Dewey's initial idea is that some experiences stand out for their richness and impact to the extent that we might later say of them, "that *was* an experience."[3] Dewey has in mind experiences such as a memorable dinner in Paris, a significant storm encountered while crossing the Atlantic (in a ship), a particularly engaging job interview, and a relationship-ending argument with a friend.[4] What makes these experiences stand out is not their subject matter but their structural components. *An* experience involves phases of doing and undergoing; it requires the awareness of the relations among these phases, as well as a developing qualitative character that runs through the experience, culminating in what Dewey calls *an* experience's consummation. Throughout this book, my approach is to take on-board only what we need from various philosophers for our purposes. This strategy leads me to interpret Dewey's view conservatively, emerging with a simplified version of his conception of *an* experience, which I will call *developed experience*.

How is this notion of developed experience useful in our project? Developed experiences are not only active but they are a particularly rich kind of active experience. I will contend that in order for an activity to be meaningful, a person must have some experiences in relation to the activity that are not passive; in fact, even recognitional experiences (which are minimally active) are insufficient. (Recognitional experiences are concerned only with identification. For example, while approaching an intersection on your bike, your experience of the stoplights is typically recognitional; you take note that the light is red, say, but you do not experience the lights in any richer sense.) I offer developed experience, then, as a kind of experience that *can* effectively contribute to meaningfulness. Importantly, once the notion of developed experience is on the table, with its detailed structure, it will not be difficult to identify precisely how certain kinds of smartphone-use can interfere with the development of experiences as well as the resulting meaningfulness.

Dewey gives us a sense of the *way* in which we experience and engage in meaningful activities. But I will contend that having developed experiences of just any object or event is insufficient for meaningfulness. Consider that one of Dewey's examples of *an* experience pertains to an illness (a bout of the grippe); there is reason to doubt that such *an* experience adds meaning to one's life. To supplement developed experience, I will draw from Albert Borgmann's writing on focal things and focal practices (Chapter 5). As I mentioned above, an example of a focal practice is a family dinner; the material anchor of that practice is the meal, which is what Borgmann calls a focal thing. I will claim that musical performance is a focal practice; the associated focal thing is a musical instrument. Like me, I expect that the reader will find the range of Borgmann's examples surprising and challenging. Here are three examples: the path of a run, such as an ocean road, is a focal thing (the focal practice is running); a fishing rod is a focal thing (the associated focal practice is fly-fishing); the wilderness is a focal thing (hiking is the focal practice).

My main claim about meaning will be that *engaging with focal things and practices by means of developed experiences can generate meaning in one's life.* I do not expect the reader to take my word for it. One interesting question to ask is: Are these philosophers' views really about meaning in life? I will support my claim that they are about meaning in life by connecting developed experiences and focal things/practices to the philosopher Susan's Wolf's "Fitting Fulfillment" theory of meaning in life (Chapter 4). You might wonder why I cannot work with only Susan Wolf's theory in this book. Her theory is too abstract for our primary purpose of uncovering the specific ways in which smartphone-distraction interferes with meaningful activities. Overcoming this shortcoming—involving Dewey and Borgmann—bears unexpected fruit.

Here is the briefest preview of Wolf's account of meaningfulness. She argues that an activity generates meaning in one's life if it satisfies both a subjective and an objective condition. For something to be meaningful, it must be subjectively fulfilling and it must be objectively valuable (this second component is what "fitting" refers to in Fitting Fulfillment). For example, playing musical instruments with others will generate meaning in one's life, (a) if one finds it fulfilling *and* (b) if this activity is valuable (or as she occasionally says, worthwhile). (Active and positive involvement in the activity are additional, required elements.) Anyone who reads such a brief description of Wolf's view will wonder what she means by subjective fulfillment and objective value. Wolf has much to say about this, which we will consider in Chapter 4. But even so, her view is abstract; for our purposes, as I have said, it must be fleshed out.

Regarding the connections to Wolf, first, I will contend that one cannot be subjectively fulfilled if one's relevant experiences are passive or merely recognitional. One *can* be subjectively fulfilled through developed experiences. Another way to approach this connection between developed experience and Wolf's subjective condition is to say that the notion of developed experience serves to flesh out the subjective condition. Importantly, the detail added to Wolf's subjective condition through developed experiences enables us to identify precisely where and how certain smartphone-use can interfere with subjective fulfillment.

In 5.7, I make the connection between focal things/practices and Wolf's *objective* condition. Wolf acknowledges that her notion of objective value is indefinite. I contend that the core of what is needed to satisfy the objective condition is that an activity must be worthwhile in a way that is independent of oneself. We will see that the substance of the argument is better served by the term "non-subjective" than it is by "objective" (Wolf occasionally employs the former term herself). This is not only to find common ground between Wolf and Borgmann, this is to flesh out Wolf's sense of worthwhileness. Even though Wolf and Borgmann operate in quite different philosophical traditions, we attain initial leverage in bringing them together through their consideration of many of the same activities—running, creating art, writing, playing music, gardening, carpentry, and so on.

Chapter 6 turns on an existential-phenomenological view of self-identity. By the time we get to this chapter, we will be able to say that a central way in which one creates one's self-identity is by engaging with focal things and practices by means of developed experiences. The shaping of one's self-identity in this way adds a certain commitment and profundity to the meaning one creates through the engagement with certain focal things and practices. If, for instance, one engages *as a drummer* in the focal practice of musical performance, this identity-work has the effect of staking one's claim on the meaning generated through this focal practice; this focal practice becomes more consequential for one than one's engagement with certain other focal practices. In light of this, it has struck me as alarming to notice that the smartphone-use *of others* can interfere with such identity-work in certain social contexts. (Incidentally, trying to understand the nature and impact of this particular kind of smartphone-distraction lit the fuse of this writing project.)

Before we get to the issues about meaning that begin in Chapter 3, in Chapter 2 I consider certain well-researched kinds of smartphone-distraction. For more than a decade, social scientists have studied smartphone-distraction as it pertains to healthcare, education, driving, and so on. I will focus on healthcare and education studies, and I will argue that this kind of research does not capture the breadth and depth of the negative effects of smartphone-distraction. I will argue that the way in which this kind of research frames smartphone-distraction prevents it from capturing the nature and effects of smartphone-distraction in relation to meaningful activities (I make this move in 2.3). We need a new approach. Importantly, Chapter 2 will also introduce some core phenomenological observations about smartphone-use which will aid us in the work we do in the remainder of the book.

Although I will continue to refer only to smartphones, much of what I say applies as well to other pieces of what I will call *intimate technologies* (2.6), such as (in addition to smartphones) smartwatches, smartglasses, and other wearables. While I am obviously critical of certain smartphone-use, in the end I will not take the position that we should turn back the clock and stop using our smartphones. My hope is that this book can contribute to a more thoughtful integration of smartphones into our lives. My intention is for my observations and arguments to be helpful in clarifying and motivating changes that we can make within our smartphone habits, as well as changes in smartphone and app design. At the end of the book (Chapter 7), I will be able to use a set of sharpened concepts to point toward a path for tackling the practical challenge of incorporating smartphones into our engagement with focal practices. Although it may come as a surprise, in the end I will suggest that certain smartphone-use may even *support* our engagement in focal practices (though I have just spoiled the surprise).

2

Distraction

2.1 Distracted Healthcare

A 56-year-old man was admitted to a teaching hospital for a routine medical procedure.[1] Following the procedure, the doctors decided to put him on the blood-thinning medication, Warfarin. The next day, after a further assessment of the man's condition, the attending physician determined that the patient should be taken off Warfarin. The case I am describing was reported by John Halamka in his article, "Order Interrupted by Text: Multitasking Mishap." When the article was written, Halamka was Chair of the U.S. Healthcare Information Technology Standards Panel. Before rejoining the story, we need a piece of context that Halamka provides: "This academic medical center had a robust computerized physician order entry (CPOE) system that allowed providers to enter orders using handheld devices and smartphones."[2]

Returning to the case now: The attending physician tells a resident (a junior doctor) to submit the order to *stop* the patient's blood-thinning medication. The resident picks up their smartphone, and begins entering the order to stop the Warfarin. While entering the order, a text message arrives from a friend with an invitation to a party. (Yes, a party.) The resident reads the text, and then writes a text message, in reply, for the purpose of RSVP-ing. Distracted by the text and reply, the resident fails to complete the order to stop the blood-thinner. Halamka explains what happened next:

> Because everyone on the team thought the medication had been stopped, no one checked the patient's INR [as explained by Halamka, the INR is a measure of anticoagulation intensity]. In addition, because of the robust CPOE system, neither the intern nor resident reviewed the medication list for the next few days so no one recognized that the patient was still receiving the Warfarin.[3]

Suspense is not one of my go-to writing tactics, so I will tell you that the patient survived—but only after emergency open-heart surgery, which was required to deal with the excess blood around his heart.[4]

The journalist who coined the term, "Distracted Doctoring," Matt Richtel, tells of a less-lucky patient, in his article, "As Doctors Use More Devices, Potential for Distraction Grows."

> Scott J. Eldredge, a medical malpractice lawyer in Denver, recently represented a patient who was left partly paralyzed after surgery. The neurosurgeon was distracted during the operation, using a wireless headset to talk on his cellphone, Mr. Eldredge said.
>
> "He was making personal calls," Mr. Eldredge said, at least 10 of them to family and business associates, according to phone records. His client's case was settled before a lawsuit was filed so there are no court records, like the name of the patient, doctor

or hospital involved. Mr. Eldredge, citing the agreement, declined to provide further details.[5]

Richtel also relates the Warfarin story in another article, "Multitasking Doctor Imperils Patient, Case Study Says."[6]

Now, there is no doubt that healthcare professionals have benefitted from the easy access that smartphones have provided to medical records, reference sources, and clinical systems, as well as the increased efficiency of communicating with colleagues and patients. Using smartphones for such purposes during working hours is referred to in the social-science literature as *on-task* smartphone-use. But, as we have just seen, healthcare professionals also use their smartphones for personal purposes while on duty; this is referred to in the literature as *off-task* use. As has just been brought home, off-task smartphone-use can distract healthcare professionals from their work.[7] In addition to individual case reports such as those above, many studies have been conducted in recent years that bear this out. The lion's share of the social-science research focuses not on doctors but on nurses and medical technicians. (Why? I will keep my guesses to myself.) As we move through this chapter, we will see that the distinction between on-task and off-task smartphone-use, while simple, is extremely useful.

Consider two studies, one of nurses, the other of nursing students. In a 2019 study based on the self-reporting of 256 nurses in Italy, "42% of nurses report that they were distracted by their use of smartphones."[8] In 2016, Sumi Cho and Eunjoo Lee conducted a survey-based study of 312 nursing students in two nursing schools in the Republic of Korea; they found that 27.9% "of the nursing students reported that they had been distracted" by smartphone-use.[9] While most of the relevant studies focus on nurses, medical technicians are also under scrutiny. One alarming result from a 2010 study of perfusionists in the United States found that 49.2% of 439 respondents reported sending text messages during cardiopulmonary bypass procedures.[10]

A concerning phenomenon that emerges in a number of these studies is that there are more incidents of distraction reported when respondents flag the distraction of their colleagues rather than their own. In Cho and Lee's study, while 27.9% of respondents reported being distracted by smartphone-use themselves, "42.9% of the respondents reported that they had witnessed other students' distraction by smartphone use."[11]

An important social aspect of smartphone-distraction that emerges from some of these studies is that respondents report being distracted by the smartphone-use of nearby others.[12] In Cho and Lee's study, for instance, "27.9% ... of the nursing students reported that they had been distracted by externally ... initiated smartphone use."[13]

There are so many studies about smartphone-distraction in healthcare that one can find articles such as a 2021 article with this title: "Smartphone distraction during nursing care: Systematic literature review."[14] The obvious is made clear in this study: a principal concern that motivates the research on smartphone-distraction in healthcare is the prospect that it can negatively affect the care of patients. In selecting studies for their review, the authors excluded "studies that deal with the use of mobile devices but not with the risk associated with their use."[15]

So, what about errors made due to smartphone-distraction? In a 2019 survey-based study of healthcare providers in emergency departments in Lebanon, Mohamad Alameddine and his colleagues found that 55% of survey respondents "reported observing their colleagues having made an error or a near miss as a result of being distracted by their SDs [smart devices]."[16] And as with the reporting of distraction generally, the negative effects of smartphone-distraction are also reported at a much higher rate by others. In a 2015 study yielding 950 respondents (members of the Academy of Medical Surgical Nurses), Deborah McBride and her colleagues considered three categories of negative effects of smartphone-use: "(1) negative performance, (2) medical errors, and (3) missed clinical information."[17] Consider the results in the following quotations from the study.

[1] A significantly lower percentage of respondents self-reported mobile phone-related performance decrements (7.4%, 61/825) than reported witnessing mobile phone-related performance decrements in other nurses (70.9%, 584/825).[18]

[2] Significantly fewer respondents self-reported making medical errors (adverse effect of care, including a near-miss or a sentinel event) because of a mobile phone-related distraction (0.8%, 7/825) than reported witnessing such medical errors in other nurses (13.1%, 108/825).[19]

[3] Likewise, significantly fewer respondents self-reported missing important clinical information because of mobile phone-related distractions (4%, 33/825) than reported witnessing other nurses missing important clinical information (29.9%, 246/825).[20]

If we can believe these reports about the performance of colleagues, this suggests that the negative effects of smartphone-use in healthcare settings are significant, and as indicated above, these effects are under-reported in self-reports.

The risks are perceived to be serious enough by the healthcare profession itself that many hospitals have developed policies aimed at curbing distraction, and some medical organizations have published position statements that include guidelines about personal technology. For example, in 2020, the Association of periOperative Registered Nurses (AORN) published a position statement entitled "Managing Distractions and Noise During Perioperative Patient Care." The statement includes the following relevant points: "During critical phases of the surgical procedure, surgical team members should create a no-interruption zone in which nonessential conversation and activities are prohibited."[21] "Distractions and noise cannot be eliminated completely from the perioperative environment; therefore, AORN is committed to advocating for a controlled environment in which distractions and noise are minimized to the greatest extent possible."[22] While the statement is focused on distractions generally, a good portion of the rationale has to do with smartphones and personal technology generally.

The American College of Surgeons (ACS) has also published a "Statement on distractions in the operating room."[23] ACS recommends that this information be included in training programs for operating-room personnel.[24] The statement begins in this way:

There are many opportunities for distraction in the operating room (OR). Some can be attributed to the introduction of new technology, such as smartphone and mobile technology, and some are a function of noise levels, unnecessary conversation, and other variables that dilute the focus of perioperative team members because their attention is drawn "to … different object[s] or different directions at the same time."[25] Because of the deleterious effects of distraction on cognitive processing and the performance of complex tasks and because of the potential impact of distraction on patient safety, it is important to recognize and mitigate the risks of distraction in the OR.[26]

Note that cognitive processing was raised in the above quotation, referring to the performance costs involved in multitasking. In subsequent sections, we will address the issue of multitasking directly.

In a section entitled, "Distractions arising from technology,"[27] ACS refers specifically to smartphones, drawing a distinction between on-task smartphone-use for accessing patient data (etc.) and off-task "undisciplined use," by which they mean use for social media, email, calls, and so on. ACS then offers guidance for smartphone-use in the OR in the form of ten considerations. They emphasize that undisciplined smartphone-use "may pose a distraction and may compromise patient care."[28] Specific guidelines include: "Whenever possible, members of the OR team, including the operating surgeon, should only engage in urgent or emergent outside communication during an operation."[29]

Smartphone-distraction in the healthcare profession is enough of a concern that hundreds of studies have been undertaken, and the results have caused numerous hospitals and healthcare organizations to publish guidelines aimed at curbing off-task smartphone-use in healthcare settings.

2.2 Distracted Education

Smartphones, tablets, and laptops have given teachers the opportunity to think anew about the ways in which they conduct their courses, and the ways students learn. Regarding smartphones in particular, there are potential pedagogical innovations that draw upon their computing power, flexibility, and portability. One innovative example of on-task smartphone-use in the classroom is the clicker app, which enables large numbers of students to weigh in on multiple-choice questions posed by a teacher during a large lecture. Students click answers in an app that is connected to the classroom's screen display. Such innovations seem positive and ostensibly harmless; they are intended to foster student engagement. But even pedagogical innovations such as using a clicker app lead to concerns about distraction: students may drift into off-task smartphone-use immediately following a bit of on-task smartphone-use.

In 2020, Sihui Ma and her colleagues conducted a study at Virginia Tech that focused on smartphone-based clickers. They uncovered something troubling: "42% of students began to use their smartphones for non-instructional [off-task] purposes immediately following the instructional episode [the on-task use], and 28% of students persisted in this behavior five minutes after the instructional episode ended."[30] This finding is concerning because it stands to reason that off-task use of smartphones in class has a negative effect on student learning. Such multitasking—engaging with a smartphone for off-task purposes while trying to learn through a lecture—comes at a cost to academic performance. This is analogous to the negative effects of off-task smartphone-use that we find in healthcare.

What about smartphone-use in education generally? In the 2020 article "Smartphone use and academic performance: A literature review," Simon Amez and his colleagues examined various studies of students at the university level, concerning "the relationship between smartphone use and academic performance."[31]

They found a "significantly negative association between smartphone use and *academic performance* in tertiary education."[32] Importantly, "no single study to date reports a positive overall association."[33]

Most of the studies reviewed by Amez and his colleagues took into consideration students' smartphone-use *in-general.* The studies were not limited to in-class smartphone-use nor were they limited to off-task use. In my view, the more interesting and concretely troubling phenomenon is smartphone-use in class, especially the psychological pull toward off-task use—whether a student is being pulled away from on-task smartphone-use toward off-task smartphone-use (as in Sihui Ma and her colleagues' clicker study) or from no smartphone-use to off-task smartphone-use. One example of such a study is Inyeop Kim and his colleagues' 2019, "Understanding Smartphone Usage in College Classrooms: A Longterm Measurement Study." They conclude that "excessive phone usage [in class] can be considered harmful to academic performance."[34]

Some studies give us a close-up, detailed view of the ways in which off-task smartphone-use affects students' behavior. Consider the 2019 study by Fritjof Sahlström and his colleagues, entitled "Connected Youth, Connected Classrooms. Smartphone Use and Student and Teacher Participation During Plenary Teaching."[35] As the title suggests, their study is focused on the effects of smartphone-use upon student participation. The researchers analyze many hours of video of student behavior, including student laptop-screen and smartphone-screen behavior. They identify two different patterns of attention and interaction in students, which they refer to as *participation frameworks.* They find that students exhibit one participation framework while they are engaged with their smartphones, and another while they are engaged with a lecture.

Sahlström and his colleagues' modest main conclusion is that "student smartphone use significantly alters participation patterns in whole-class interaction."[36] One practical implication is that students who engage in off-task smartphone-use are less effective at class-participation: "[W]e have evidence of lag in the student uptake of sequential turn-taking cues when students are using their phones. In practice, this means that student hand-raising and self-selection occurs with a slight but significant delay, resulting in not being able to secure the next turn at talk."[37]

Modest as their claims are, this study offers us an interesting and detailed glimpse of the scattershot character of multitasking between (a) off-task smartphone-use and (b) attending to a lecture/taking notes. I want to consider the researchers' description of what they say is representative of one kind of common phone-use pattern.[38] The student at issue, Malin, is watching/listening to her History teacher and taking notes on her laptop. The researchers write: "We use her interaction in this History lesson to exemplify, introduce and open up some of the most pervasive features of connected classroom participation in our material."[39] In reading their account, I am reminded that taking notes in class is difficult! Watching and listening to a teacher while taking notes requires frequent shifts of attention and varied cognitive work. But one aspect of this work that makes it feasible is that the focus is on the same content in listening/watching the teacher and note-taking. A fascinating result of their analysis is that ordinary listening/watching and note-taking seems to be supported by a regular attentional rhythm. Smartphone-use throws off this rhythm.

When taking notes, her [Malin's] gaze follows a seesaw pattern, with two to five seconds spent looking at the teacher and the board, followed by a similar amount of time with her gaze turned to her laptop screen. This gaze pattern is distinctly different from the way the students attend to their smartphones, where there is generally an extended focus on the phone, interspersed with briefer glances at the teacher.[40]

Here is an extended quotation describing the addition of a smartphone into the already-difficult task of watching and listening to a teacher while taking notes. The reader will notice the disruption to the rhythm as well as the striking shift in subject matter between the content of the lecture and the topics the student engages with on her phone.

Malin has typed most of the way through a list of countries constituting the iron curtain when there is a notification on the smartphone screen of a Snapchat message arriving, right at the end of having typed "Albania" on the laptop. She gazes briefly at the smartphone screen, but continues typing until reaching the end of the list of the countries to be typed out. ... After she has typed the name of the last country, Czechoslovakia, the teacher's projector screen momentarily goes blank. This is commented on by the teacher, saying, "Sorry, it will soon return." Precisely at the beginning of the teacher's turn, Malin reaches for her smartphone, picks it up, places it behind her laptop screen [so that the teacher cannot see the phone] and opens the chat message from her friend, Markus. In between clicking the notification and beginning reading, she turns her gaze to the teacher in the time it takes for the message to open up. When she returns her gaze to the phone, she reads a new message in a sustained discussion on whether her school is a stuck-up-school or not, with her friend asking … whether Malin felt hurt when he dissed her school … This is the beginning of a sustained sequence lasting two minutes and ten seconds where Malin's gaze is turned to her phone, and where she is chatting with Markus. She takes seven seconds to compose and send her first message (out of four). … While composing her message the teacher says, to the whole class, "Here is the new Europe after the Second World War." We have no evidence of Malin attending to the teacher's talk. She continues with a second message, which takes 27 s to compose.[41]

The researchers emphasize that students use smartphones in the classroom primarily to communicate socially with others outside of the classroom.

The two minutes of Malin's phone use is typical of the students' phone use in the project material, both in the Finnish and Swedish corpus. It exemplifies the largest and most substantial change following the introduction of mobile devices in classrooms: the wide, varied and easily available access to social interaction for students. In the material, student phone use in classrooms is predominantly for direct or indirect communication with others. Almost all of this interaction takes place with people or communities outside the classroom.[42]

It is accounts like this one that lead me to believe that anyone who attempts to argue that off-task smartphone-use in class does not negatively affect academic performance is waging an uphill battle. The detailed descriptions of the scattershot behavior of students such as those offered by Sahlström and his colleagues lends support to the notion that off-task smartphone-use in class has a negative impact on academic performance. (Although it is not a primary goal in what follows, the next two sections will deepen support for this claim.)

2.3 Means and Ends

The approach taken in the kinds of social-science studies we have just encountered will not help us to understand the nature and effects of smartphone-distraction upon meaningful activities, projects, and experiences. The problem is not that such researchers are simply focused on the wrong activities. That is, my point is not that such studies fall short because they do not focus upon musical performances, festive dinners, hiking, and so on. Instead, my contention will be that the orientation and methods employed in such studies would prove ineffective in studying smartphone-distraction in a wide range of meaningful activities. (In fact, even regarding some activities that are already studied by these researchers, such as classroom activities, in Chapter 6 we will see why the potential meaningfulness of these activities falls through the cracks of such studies.)

Why will the approach taken in studies such as those we encountered not help us to understand smartphone-distraction from meaningful activities? Simply put, the researchers who conduct such studies *frame* the phenomena they are investigating by drawing a distinction between means and ends. In addition, both means and ends are understood to be quantifiable. Notice that in the studies we have considered, the impact of smartphone-distraction is understood in terms of interference within a means, the impact of which is cashed out in terms of an effect on an end.

I mean *cashed out* in two senses: First, the impact of smartphone-distraction (i.e., why the distraction matters) is interpreted in terms of an effect on an end. Second, the smartphone-distraction is *made sense of* (rendered intelligible) in terms of the effect on an end.

We can detect this approach in the way the studies emphasize quantifiable ends. In the healthcare research, smartphone-distraction is cashed out in terms of worse patient treatment (an end). In the education research, smartphone-distraction is cashed out in terms of worse academic performance, often measured through exams (an end). The general approach taken is that if smartphone-use negatively affects the effective completion of a given task, then this is the core of the concern about smartphone-use and distraction.

To put this differently, the studies discussed in the previous sections pull processes (means) apart from outcomes (ends), analyzing and measuring them separately. Means and ends are treated as isolable components of an activity. By framing the concern with smartphone-distraction in this way, the smartphone-distraction that negatively affects certain kinds of meaningful activities falls through the cracks. How so? Some meaningful activities cannot be accurately understood or assessed by being carved up in this way, into means and ends.

The explanation I just offered was abstract. A preview of Albert Borgmann's writing on focal things and practices (Chapter 5) will give the reader a sense of what I have in mind. Here is an example of a meaningful activity from which smartphones can distract us, but concerning which we tend to be unclear about the character and impact of the distraction. A family dinner, or a festive meal with friends, can be meaningful. But notice that we cannot accurately understand such an activity nor its meaningfulness by conceiving of it in terms of means and ends. How would we divide such a dinner into means and ends? Would the end be eating? Even seemingly marginal aspects such as helping the cook to prepare the meal can be meaningful; the conversation around the table can certainly be meaningful—even the clean-up can foster solidarity in a meaningful way.[43] The problem is that potential meaningfulness permeates the entire activity, even some aspects that we might take to be means are meaningful.

Notice how much more straightforward it is to make sense of why smartphone-distraction is a problem for a perfusionist during a bypass procedure: one can hypothesize deleterious effects on patient care, based on which one can devise a study that quantifies the performance cost. Many meaningful activities are unlike this kind of case because they involve the intertwining of means and ends that we recognize in the example of a family dinner (for more on this general notion, see 5.3.1 and 5.7).

To take another example, consider playing guitar, which is meaningful not merely for the music you make (the end) but also for the process of playing itself, the development of skills, the cultivation of meaningful connections to music of the past, and so on. If we expand this example to include making music with others, dimensions of meaning are extended. If we further expand the example to involve musical performance, the opportunities for meaningfulness are additionally extended (I develop this example in Chapter 5).

We will expand upon the following ideas in Chapters 3 and 6 but I raise these issues here in order to flag for the reader that we could also draw upon the views of John Dewey and Hubert Dreyfus to identify the limitations in the ways in which the previous studies analyze smartphone-distraction. In Chapter 3, I will focus on what

John Dewey calls "*an* experience," extracting a more limited conception which I call *developed experience*. We will see that means cannot be separated from ends if we are to correctly understand developed experiences. Developed experiences are completed in a way that is not merely an end, it is a consummation. Each developed experience has what Dewey calls a pervasive quality which is present incipiently in all of the experience's phases, as well as in the consummation. Thomas Alexander explains why these components cannot be analyzed as isolable means and ends: "Each phase or movement [of the experience] must be grasped *as* a phase or part of a larger whole; the sense of the whole must be present in the part."[44] If we were to conceive of the smartphone-distraction from developed experiences as merely an interference with the means, this would be to misunderstand the structure of this kind of experience. We cannot adequately understand the ways in which smartphone-distraction can interfere with developed experiences through a means/ends analysis. Alexander elaborates this by discussing an artwork, but what he says here applies to all developed experiences:

> The sense of the consummatory, therefore, is present throughout *an* experience and is felt intensely in the guiding, unifying, organizing quality through which all the parts belong and cooperate toward the overall end. The sense of the consummatory is gradually transformed from a feeling of immanent possibility, of the ideal capacity of the experience, to one of progressive realization. The end of the work [the work of art] does not lie outside it but within it as a moving force, the entelechy rather than the terminus. "A, drama or a novel," Dewey dryly observes, "is not the final sentence."[45]

Dewey makes the point in this way: "Fulfilling, consummating, are continuous functions [of *an* experience], not mere ends, located at one place only … The form of the whole is therefore present in every member [every component of *an* experience]."[46] I return to these issues in 3.7.

We could even argue against the effectiveness of a means/ends analysis for understanding smartphone-distraction from meaningfulness from the perspective of Chapter 6, where I consider the work one does to create one's self-identity, from an existential-phenomenological perspective. Hubert Dreyfus makes the point we need here while discussing the self-identity of a college professor. He ultimately conceives of self-identity as self-interpretation, which cannot be understood as an end or goal that is, or is not, achieved (such as being promoted to full professor). Instead, self-identity is a continual self-interpretation. For this reason, in his 2007 lectures on Heidegger's *Being and Time*, Dreyfus remarks that calling this self-interpretation "professor" may be misleading because it gives the impression of being an objective one can achieve. He prefers "teacher."[47] Therefore, we have a similar problem as above with a means/ends analysis. We cannot neatly carve the shaping of one's self-identity into means and ends for the purpose of characterizing smartphone-distraction in terms of its deleterious effects on an end.

Neither the activities I describe as meaningful in future chapters nor the nature and effects of the relevant smartphone-distraction can be grasped in terms of a means/ends analysis. (For a callback and elaboration of this point, see 5.7.)

Consider the following practical concerns. Many parents struggle to persuade their children not to use their smartphones during dinner. In some families, the situation may be reversed.[48] How can we talk about this issue of smartphone-distraction constructively? Similarly, how should musicians and audience members think and talk about the use of smartphones by the latter during a performance? What should teachers and students take into consideration when discussing smartphone-use in the classroom? In these and related cases, my contention is that we should frame this discussion in terms of meaningfulness, not in terms of means and ends, not on the model of the distracted perfusionist. This is a practical ambition of the book. I address this again in 5.8, and the theme is deepened in Chapter 6.

Before we turn to the chapters in which we consider meaningfulness directly (Chapters 3–6), we need to sharpen our understanding of multitasking, as well as our understanding of the ways in which smartphones operate in our experience and comportment. In order to do so, we will be lingering in a more or less means/ends orientation for the remainder of this chapter.

2.4 Multitasking

When I discuss smartphone-distraction with students, some acknowledge that off-task smartphone-use in class may negatively affect academic performance; other students are of the opinion that their extensive experience with multitasking enables them to manage such situations well. The latter idea is that they can pay attention to what is happening in class in addition to, occasionally, paying attention to what is happening within their smartphones.

Some social scientists who write about smartphone-distraction claim that there is no such thing as *true* multitasking. For example, in her chapter, "Distractions in the Operating Room," Michelle Feil writes:

> Unfortunately, there is a very real limit to the ability of the human brain to multitask. True multitasking refers to performing two tasks simultaneously. This is something the human brain is not able to do. What the brain is actually doing in these situations is task switching. Each time the brain switches between tasks, it distracts from the primary task and may contribute to error.[49]

The phenomenon of multitasking turns out to be a bit more complex than this. It will be fruitful for us briefly to explore some of these complexities.

Performing two tasks simultaneously, which Feil calls "true multitasking," is what psychologists call *dual-task performance*. The other phenomenon is *serial task-switching*. Both phenomena are referred to as multitasking in the psychology literature. The prevailing view of psychologists is that we have cognitive processing limits that generally result in performance costs when we are engaged in either kind of multitasking (dual-task performance or serial task-switching).[50]

Given this, it is surprising to learn that some psychologists have found certain kinds of dual-task performance to be possible. And in some cases, they find that there is little or no performance cost. One explanation for this is that a certain pair of tasks which are initially separated can become integrated. As Irwing Koch and his colleagues express the point: "The processes of performing the two initially separate tasks become intertwined in a way that allow them to be performed conjointly."[51] This integration, if it can be achieved, eliminates the processing limitation, which is often metaphorically described by psychologists as a cognitive *bottleneck*.[52] In order for this integration to occur, practice with the tasks is required. Relatedly, a person might become so familiar with certain tasks that the tasks become, to some degree, automatic.[53] Once we are made aware of these details, this sort of dual-task performance is perhaps less surprising, because the resulting integrated task does not seem to be a case of "true multitasking," as I can imagine Feil pointing out.

For our purposes, it is helpful to consider real-world examples of multitasking, rather than experimentally contrived tasks. Regarding the following real-world examples, I can justifiably call them cases of multitasking, but I cannot definitively say whether they are cases of dual-task performance or task-switching. We will see that this does not matter for our purposes; we need a different distinction, which the philosopher of technology Diane Michelfelder provides.

A fruitful train of thought emerges in the philosophy of technology, beginning with a discussion of *multi-attention*. We will see that we can treat multi-attention and multitasking as equivalent (at least for our purposes). Galit Wellner raises the thought-provoking example of driving a car while having a conversation with a physically present passenger.[54] This kind of multitasking has obviously been common for many decades. That this is an example of successful multitasking is made even more likely when we imagine, as Michelfelder suggests, that the driving is taking place on a country road. Many of us have had the experience of engaging in even a challenging conversation with a passenger while driving effectively—as long as the driving is taking place in an environment that presents few driving challenges. Consider also the somewhat similar multitasking example of folding laundry while watching television. In such cases, when a folding challenge, or a driving challenge, emerges, we momentarily direct our attention away from the television-watching or passenger-conversation in order to deal with the challenge. We can see from these examples that even though the term "multi-attention" is being used here, this is multitasking;[55] these cases involve perceptual attention, cognition, and action.[56] (Below, I will continue to refer to this as "multi-attention," rather than multitasking, only while discussing the philosophers who write about multi-attention.)

Let's remain with the writing about multi-attention for a few more paragraphs. Michelfelder draws a distinction that we can put to good use, between *weak* multi-attention and *strong* multi-attention. Roughly speaking, weak multi-attention is cognitively less demanding; strong multi-attention is cognitively more demanding. If we imagine driving on a country road, a case in which driving is not very cognitively demanding, then driving while speaking to a physically present passenger—or even speaking on a phone, according to Michelfelder—is arguably a case of weak multi-attention. More precisely, according to Michelfelder, multi-attention is weak when two activities are *complementary*, when we can combine two activities into one single object of focus, such as driving and talking or folding laundry while watching television. The point for us to take away is that weak multi-attention—we can call this *weak multitasking*—seems common and viable.

Multi-attention (or multitasking) is strong when the two activities are not complementary, and when we cannot combine two activities into one single object of focus. As Michelfelder puts it, with a slightly different spin, "Strong multi-attention could be defined as the simultaneous attention given to more than one object where the attention given to one object does not improve the experience of the other."[57] She offers these vivid examples:

> Using one hand to steer a vacuum cleaner across the floor while using the other to brush one's teeth, or playing bike polo while looking at an iPhone attached to the handlebars of one's bike to keep track of how the stock market is doing, would be examples of strong multi-attention.[58]

For our purposes, two conclusions are important. First, weak multitasking is feasible (e.g., driving on a country road while having a conversation). Psychologists maintain that practice is a key contributor to one becoming able to multitask in this way. But more importantly, regarding smartphone multitasking, the kinds of cases we are interested in—which involve smartphone-use such as having a text conversation—seem to be cases of *strong* multi-attention (strong multitasking). Strong-multitasking comes at a cost to performance. These real-world cases of strong multitasking seem to be examples of serial multitasking. If this is what Feil had in mind, then she turns out to be right in the end.

Consider the case documented by Sahlström and his colleagues in which a student is attempting to follow a lecture/taking notes while also texting with a friend (2.2). This is strong multitasking. We saw the back-and-forth nature of this activity that is emblematic of task-switching. This would be even worse if the class activity involved trying to understand the way in which a particular philosophical argument fits together, where more active, sustained cognitive work is required. Or consider the case of the perfusionist engaged in a cardiopulmonary bypass procedure while having a text conversation. These cases are more like using one hand to steer a vacuum cleaner across the floor while using the other to brush one's teeth than they are like talking on the phone while driving on a country road. Texting while following a lecture or texting while being engaged in a bypass procedure are contradictory activities, not complementary activities—they require strong multitasking, not weak multitasking.

Regarding the philosophy class example, philosophical reasoning requires holding multiple points in one's mind for extended periods of time. While a given argument is explained in class, allowing one's focus to be pulled away can be disastrous. Missing one inferential maneuver, for instance, can sever a pivotal connection in one's understanding of the reasoning at issue, making it unlikely that one comes to understand the argument. Even if certain kinds of multitasking can be performed without costs (weak multitasking), the kinds of smartphone-distraction cases we are concerned with cannot be performed without costs, or at least this will be my contention. Incidentally, when more studies are conducted that focus on off-task smartphone-use in classrooms, the Sahlström study, as well as what we have learned about strong multitasking, suggest that off-task use will be found to negatively affect academic performance. (A reminder: we are lingering in a means/ends orientation, sharpening some distinctions and introducing new concepts; we are not yet considering meaningfulness.)

2.5 Other Distractions, Sedimentation

We have seen evidence that off-task smartphone-use by healthcare workers can have a negative impact on patient care. And we have seen that there is likely a performance cost when students use smartphones for off-task purposes in class. I have supplemented this evidence by employing the distinction between strong and weak multitasking, and I have suggested that these examples likely involve activities that are not complementary; they involve strong multitasking (e.g., dispensing medicine while texting with a friend or engaging with social media while listening to a lecture). Where there is strong multitasking, in other words, there are likely performance costs.

Let's remain in the classroom for a moment. I imagine a reader having the reasonable thought that there have always been distractions in classrooms, such as doodling, daydreaming, and whispered comments, as there have been distractions in various other situations as well. *Why all the fuss about smartphone-distraction?* In response to this, the first thing I say is that it is important to reflect on the impact of smartphone-use now because we are experiencing a dramatic increase in smartphone-use in many contexts (we are not experiencing a dramatic increase in doodling). As smartphones increasingly insert themselves into our lives, we should seek to understand their impact. Examining the effects of smartphone-use is pressing.

But is smartphone-distraction different from doodling, daydreaming, and whispered comments? Smartphone-distraction is different from many other kinds of distraction in that most other distractive objects do not pull at our attention in the same way, to the same degree, and with the same frequency. Doodling, for instance, does not pull at one's attention in the way that a text conversation does. Whispered comments are perhaps more demanding of attention than doodling, but typically they require less attention than a text conversation. And importantly, a single text conversation is only one of many enticements in our phones that pull at our attention.

We can employ the distinction between strong and weak multitasking to point to one way in which smartphone-distraction is particularly problematic. Having a text conversation on a smartphone tends to be less complementary to classroom engagement than doodling, daydreaming, and even whispered comments. Doodling while engaging with a lecture typically requires only weak multitasking, something like driving on a country road while having a conversation. If this is granted, then we can say that, typically, doodling (and perhaps occasional daydreaming and whispered comments as well) will not prevent individuals from remaining engaged in a class, and so will not come with a significant cost to academic performance. Of course, ultimately, to settle the issue we would need to consider just how much whispering and daydreaming are at issue. Is the whispering limited to the occasional comment or is it an extended conversation? I will strengthen the case about the uniqueness of smartphone-distraction below by considering the phenomenon of sedimentation and by describing the intimacy of smartphones.

What about the use of other potentially distracting technological devices, such as laptops? Here is a fork in the road. I could broaden my focus and consider the standard category of personal technology, arguing that smartphones and laptops present some similar challenges, some different. Indeed, regarding the classroom example, we can point to studies which conclude that students are distracted into off-task laptop-use resulting in performance costs.[59] But rather than go down this road, I want to draw a distinction between smartphones and laptops. I will begin to offer support for drawing this distinction in the remainder of this chapter. Smartphones are phenomenologically different from laptops; we experience and engage with smartphones in ways that are importantly different. As a result, we will see that smartphones are particularly distracting.

As we take another step toward understanding smartphones and their potential to distract, it will help to consider a basic structural feature of experience. Our experience has a structure at least in the sense that some things are in the foreground and others are in the background.[60] Take the example of a perfusionist engaged in a cardiopulmonary bypass procedure. When a perfusionist is focused on her work, in the foreground of her experience are the relevant screens displaying information relevant to the patient's status, and the patient himself. In the background are phenomena such as a conversation in the hall.

Now, let's say that the perfusionist receives a text message from a friend, and begins to engage in a text conversation on her smartphone, which consists of sending and receiving a few text messages. During this text conversation, what was previously in the foreground of her perception suddenly recedes into the background. The person with whom the technician is now texting, and that person's thoughts and questions, surge into the foreground. The perfusionist becomes engaged with her texting friend, and the friend is experienced as "nearer" than the patient she is supposed to be monitoring, even if her friend is 6,000 miles away.[61] If this is right, then the perfusionist disengages (to some significant degree) from her immediate context while texting, insofar as her immediate context recedes into the background. The perfusionist has been experientially somewhat removed from the context in which she is working.

One might expect that considering this difference in perceptual structures would convince the perfusionist that she cannot successfully multitask in this way. But perhaps the perfusionist would persist in her belief that she can control her attention in order to effectively shift back and forth between the texts and the relevant monitors rapidly, and at will. This shifting enables her, she might claim, to give sufficient attention both to her texting and to the relevant data.

I have already objected to such a claim by contending that what is at issue here is strong multitasking, which comes with a cost to performance. Next, I want to strengthen my argument while simultaneously beginning to make the case that smartphones should be distinguished from laptops in such considerations.

The foreground/background structure of experience is a very general experiential structure. We can speculate about other, more specific ways in which our experience is structured. Some philosophers of technology claim that certain pieces of technology shape our perceptual experience in one way or another. For example, Robert Rosenberger points out that when we speak on a phone, we typically do not experience the properties of the phone itself (its weight, materials, design, etc.); rather, the phone becomes transparent; we primarily experience the substance of the conversation and the person with whom we are speaking.[62] This piece of technology gives a structure to our experience; when we pick up a phone and begin speaking, our experience immediately becomes structured in this particular way.

The sociologist Jane Vincent makes a related point, by emphasizing the flip side of this structure. When we pick up a call, not only is it the case that our focus is on the conversation and the person with whom we are speaking—our focus is no longer on our physical surroundings, which Vincent refers to as the "co-present." She puts it this way: "The behaviours displayed while the mobile phone is being used have less regard to the co-present, but rather it is the absent-present, the people who are connected to the user via their mobile phone, who are dominant."[63]

We are considering the ways in which our perceptual experience is given a shape, a structure, by smartphones. The next issue to consider is how "sticky," so to speak, these structures are. How much control do we have over these structures? You can see why this is important if you consider the perfusionist's objection to my concern above. The perfusionist suggests that she can control her attention in order to effectively shift back and forth, at will, between the texting and the relevant patient-monitors. Rosenberger applies Maurice Merleau-Ponty's general concept of *sedimentation* to our experience with technology, claiming that the experiential structures associated with certain pieces of technology are deeply engrained through habitual use (i.e., sticky indeed). He writes,

> Sedimentation refers to the strength of the habits associated with the experiential structures of a given human-technology relation. It is the magnitude of the habitual force associated with a user's relationship with a particular technology. When a particular human-technology relation has a high degree of sedimentation, that user is strongly inclined to experience the use of that technology in a specific, long-established manner.[64]

Whether we are considering speaking on the phone or texting, we can make the same point. When the perfusionist begins to text, the experiential structure that is commonly associated with her texting activity automatically and immediately clicks into gear; this is a structure in which the text-conversation is in the foreground.

We can unpack the sedimentation metaphor further: "like rock formations built up over time through the accumulation of small deposits" of sediment, the persisting structure of the perfusionist's texting experience is constructed from all of the many times she texts—on her couch, in bed, on the bus, walking, and so on.[65] Since the structure is constructed of so many "deposits," this experiential structure that is associated with texting is stubborn, sticky; it is not easily altered. If one's relationship to smartphones is truly this stubborn, then it seems unlikely that the perfusionist will have the requisite control to enable her to make the requisite shifts in attention; it is unlikely that she could text and remain effectively engaged with the responsibilities of the bypass procedure. It is likely, then, that the perfusionist's experiential structure associated with texting disengages her from the context of the procedure—while texting, she is pulled out of the bypass context and transported into a texting orientation. This rigid and specific experiential structure is a part of what makes the perfusionist's situation a case of strong multitasking. The shifting back and forth is more difficult and costly than the perfusionist is aware.

We can put a finer point on the stubbornness of experiential structures by employing the concept of *dominant stability*, which invites us to think about the combination of a smartphone's (or an app's) design, habits of use, as well as sedimentation.[66] We can now read the full Rosenberger quotation, which includes his point from above. In what follows, he is describing dominant stability through the example of a cell phone, in the context of his analysis of driving while speaking on a cell.

It is important to recognize that our typical relationship to the telephone . . . should be understood as the telephone's "dominant stability." That is, the dominant way users experience the phone is as a device which itself takes on a degree of transparency as it is used, and which composes a user's overall awareness into a field [a structure] primarily and centrally occupied by the content of the conversation and the presence of the interlocutor. By "dominant stability," two things are indicated: (1) that this is the typical usage of the phone, the one for which the device was designed, and the one which the user typically intends to take up; and (2) that the habits associated with this stability are deeply sedimented through a user's individual history of usage.[67]

If we follow this reasoning, we encounter a disagreement with Michelfelder: there is an important difference between (a) having a conversation with a physically present passenger while driving, and (b) having a conversation over the phone while driving.[68]

Smartphones are even more likely than some other pieces of technology—such as laptops—to possess a quite specific dominant stability, because smartphone design, and the way we tend to use smartphones, results in their occupying an intimate space in our lives. Smartphones are more intimate than traditional telephones or laptops. The thought is that the dominant stability of a smartphone, being established through use as an intimate device, is quite likely to pull one away from a physical environment, and to pull the user into the world of her smartphone in a way that is sedimented and difficult to control. Note also that we are not typically aware of these structures nor their rigidity. For our purposes, the point is that a smartphone's dominant stability makes it quite difficult for the perfusionist not to be distracted from the bypass procedure once a text conversation begins. The situation is similar for the student texting in a classroom (recall the distractive behavior of students in the study of Sahlström and his colleagues in 2.2). Dominant stability and sedimentation are features of smartphone engagement that help to explain why multitasking that involves smartphone-use such as texting is strong, rather than weak. In the next section, I will add support to the claim that smartphones are unlike laptops; smartphones are intimate technologies rather than personal technologies.

2.6 Personal vs. Intimate Technology

Years ago, when we began referring to desktop and laptop computers as "personal technology," we had no way of anticipating just how personal certain new technological devices would become. Desktops and laptops are not *as personal* as smartphones and wearables, such as smartwatches and smartglasses.[69] We need a term for referring to these more personal, *closely* personal kinds of technologies. I will refer to these as *intimate technologies*. I will focus explicitly on smartphones but much of what I say will also apply to wearable technologies.

There are lines of investigation in the social sciences that lend support to the claim that smartphones are intimate technologies, setting them apart from desktops and laptops. To begin, perhaps what creates the opening for smartphones to become more personal than laptops is simply their portability and variable functionality. (In the healthcare research on smartphone-distraction, some researchers distinguish between laptops and smartphones in terms of portability, and the researchers have then connected portability to increased distractive potential.[70]) Technologists were beginning to note the unusually personal nature of cell phones early in the century. In 2005, Lara Srivastava wrote, "Indeed, users are getting closer and closer to their mobile phone and at all times of the day. A large number of people use their mobile phones as their alarm clock and sleep with their phone under their pillow or on their bedside table."[71] A 2018 PEW report found that most people interact with their phones the first thing in the morning. Seventy-two percent of teens at least sometimes "check for messages or notifications as soon as they wake up."[72] Older teens (ages fifteen to seventeen) are "particularly likely" to engage in this morning ritual. We know that smartphones provide myriad opportunities for social connectedness, which must be an important factor in why we began to feel emotionally attached to our smartphones,[73] as Srivastava says:

> The mobile phone has indeed become the most *intimate* aspect of a user's personal sphere of objects (e.g. keys, wallet, money, etc.). It gives users the impression that they are constantly connected to the world outside, and therefore less alone. Both physical and emotional attachment to mobile handsets is increasing.[74]

One way that researchers have revealed the degree to which even earlier mobile phones became intimate objects is through the observation that a wide range of users undergo anxiety upon being separated from their phones. In 2014, the media psychologist Nancy Cheever and her colleagues wrote: "With the majority of American adults using smartphones on a daily basis ... people's dependence on these devices has created a culture of connectedness in which users access their WMDs [wireless mobile devices] everywhere and at any time."[75] Cheever and her colleagues investigated the effects of separating individuals from their smartphones. The associated article's long title conveys their focus: "Out of sight is not out of mind: The impact of restricting wireless mobile device use on anxiety levels among low, moderate and high users." Their contention is that the effect of separating moderate and heavy users from their smartphones should be conceived as a form of separation anxiety:

> While anxiety is a symptom of substance withdrawal, researchers have been unable to clearly classify WMD overuse or dependency as an addiction. A more appropriate classification might be separation anxiety ... whereby moderate to heavy WMD users experience a feeling of loss when their device is absent. Separation anxiety is a salient feature of most close relationships. Because many people rely on their WMD for communication, entertainment, information, and to stay connected to loved ones and acquaintances, the WMD may have become a surrogate friend or family member that satisfies people's needs and desires. When the device is taken away or even placed out of sight, people who rely on this technology more will undoubtedly feel separation anxiety or "lost" without it.[76]

If Cheever and her colleagues are correct—if moderate and heavy users of smartphones experience separation anxiety upon being separated from their smartphones—then this emotional connection to smartphones is another kind of justification for referring to smartphones as intimate technologies.

In 2011, the sociologist Jane Vincent found that individuals considered their mobile phones to be very personal possessions; they felt different about landlines, laptops, and so on. One reason mobile phones are experienced as personal devices is, again, portability; we carry mobile phones with us almost always. It is also important that even when our ringers are silenced, information from friends and loved ones flows into our phone. This information can be accessed quickly and easily. Vibrating notifications of incoming calls and other information makes us feel connected even when our phone is silenced. Vincent goes a step further, highlighting that it is comforting simply knowing that your phone is with you, that it is collecting information and maintaining your contact with the outside world.[77]

Similar to Cheever and her colleagues' conclusion a few years later, Vincent flags the negative emotions associated with not having one's phone: "For these respondents there is a sense of vulnerability about not having their mobile phone. ... they just have to have the phone with them or else they feel uncomfortable and strange, even isolated."[78] Some respondents said that they felt "lost," "naked," or "could not cope" without their phones.[79] What is fascinating here is that Vincent seems to be describing something like alienation or estrangement brought on by the absence of a mobile phone. Vincent finds that, for some of her respondents, having access to the internet, and so on, through a computer, does not fill the void of a missing mobile phone.[80] Again, here, we see that the distinction is drawn explicitly between personal computers and even the earlier mobile phones. "The mobile phone for these respondents was more than merely a tool for communications—it had come to represent much more. It elicited positive and negative emotion responses ... causing them distress and anxiety if they forgot or lost it."[81] Years later, a 2018 PEW report found that 56% of teens experience a negative emotion, such as anxiety or loneliness, when their phones are absent.[82]

As we have progressed from more limited mobile phones to smartphones, the multiplying features and functionality provide more and more kinds of connection between me and others, and between me and my smartphone. Consider the intimate nature of differently vibrating notifications for different friends and family members. In this case, we *feel* contact with specific others even while our phones are silenced and in our pockets. I am contending that the intimate nature of smartphones distinguishes them from laptops sufficiently to warrant treating smartphones separately. And regarding the observations in 2.5, the intimacy of smartphones lends support to the claim that our use of smartphones involves sedimentation, and lends support to the claim that many uses of smartphones, when mixed with other activities, should be regarded as strong multitasking.

2.7. Taking Stock

Social scientists have conducted much research on smartphone-distraction among healthcare professionals (2.1). They find that personal use of smartphones at work (off-task use) is a distraction that has negative effects on patient care, including occasionally the making of medical errors. The research also shows that healthcare workers are distracted by the smartphone-use of other healthcare workers. As a result of the concern about smartphone-distraction, some hospitals and medical organizations have published guidelines intended to curb distraction. In light of what we have considered, we can extend the meaning of off-task use: even if one is using one's smartphone to do something generally related to work, it is reasonable to classify the use as off-task when it is not relevant to the particular task at-hand. If, for instance, a doctor is examining a patient while simultaneously having a text conversation with another patient, for our purposes, this texting should be categorized as off-task smartphone-use.

A similar structure of concern emerges in research on smartphones in education settings (2.2). There is some evidence that smartphone-use in the classroom comes at a cost to academic performance. One study that gives us a sense of the distractive power of smartphones discovered that after instructor-prompted on-task smartphone-use, a significant percentage of students began using their smartphones for off-task purposes. We also considered a study by Sahlström and his colleagues that gives us a vivid picture of the moment-to-moment mechanisms of smartphone-distraction.

The orientation and methods employed in studies such as those discussed in 2.1 and 2.2 will not enable us to elucidate the nature and effects of smartphone-distraction upon meaningful projects, activities, and experiences. The principal reason for this is that the researchers who conduct such studies frame the phenomena they are investigating by drawing a distinction between means and ends (2.3). Their approach ultimately reduces our understanding and concern with smartphone-distraction to a matter of performance costs vis-à-vis tasks. We can see the core of the problem by considering one of Borgmann's examples of a focal practice, a family dinner. It is ineffective to attempt to make sense of smartphone-distraction in terms of a negative effect on an end (eating, say) because potential elements of meaningfulness permeate the activity. In 2.3, I also noted that this means/ends critique can be extracted from the philosophical orientations of Chapters 3 and 6.

In 2.3 I introduced a practical challenge that this book should address. While participating in focal practices, and while having developing experiences, the best reason to remain engaged in the practice or experience (and to avoid smartphone-distraction) has to do with fostering meaning. I will attempt to make the case that this reasoning is more effective, in some cases, than reasons based on the effective performance of tasks (5.8 and Chapters 6 and 7).

One skeptical view of multitasking is that there is no such thing (2.4). When a person believes that she is multitasking, what she is really doing is rapidly switching back-and-forth between or among tasks. In this sort of case, there is clearly a cost to performance. But in one sense, the reality is more complex. It turns out that pairs of tasks can be more or less compatible, even complementary in certain cases. Compatible tasks can be integrated in a way that allows a person to perform both tasks simultaneously, likely with little or no performance cost. Call this *weak multitasking* ("weak" because it is cognitively less demanding than *strong multitasking*). Strong multitasking comes with a cost to performance insofar as it involves tasks that are not compatible, not complementary (these distinctions are Diane Michelfelder's, although she uses the term "multi-attention"). I contend that the cases of smartphone-distraction that concern us, pertaining to meaningful activities, are instances of strong multitasking. The off-task smartphone-use we encountered in the research on healthcare and education are also cases of strong multitasking. For our purposes in Chapter 3 and beyond, our concern will not be that strong multitasking comes at a cost to task-performance but that *strong multitasking negatively affects developing experiences, which negatively affects engagement with focal things and practices.*

One reason that the smartphone-uses that interest us here are accurately characterized as strong multitasking has to do with our experiential relationship to our phones, or we might say, with more scope, *the phenomenology of smartphones* (2.5 and 2.6). Our experiential orientation to our phones is shaped by our many engagements with the phone. For example, one straightforward experiential structure is that, while on a voice call, we attend to the person with whom we are speaking more than to our physical surroundings. A similar experiential structure emerges as we engage with a text conversation. Such structures are stubborn, sticky, sedimented through repetition. This stubbornness is one reason why it is difficult to imagine how one could make texting while listening to a lecture (say) an instance of weak multitasking (that is, make them into compatible activities). The stubbornness of smartphone experiential structures makes them difficult to alter at will. And, many of the structures pull the smartphone-user out of her physical environment.

The experiential structures we establish with our smartphones, and the rigidity of these structures, point to a difference between smartphones and laptops. One way to capture this difference is to say that laptops are a personal technology; smartphones are an intimate technology (2.6). To support this claim, we can appeal to social scientists who have observed that smartphone users treat their smartphones (and not their laptops) as one of a very small cluster of objects that they cannot do without, to the point of undergoing anxiety upon separation from their smartphones.

In the next chapter, by drawing upon John Dewey's writing on experience, we will begin to develop a conception of active experience that will enable us to better understand the kind of engagement required to foster meaning in life. And we will lay a detailed foundation that will enable us to explicate the ways in which smartphone-use can distract us from the cultivation of this meaningfulness.

3

Developed Experience

3.1 Experience

We should not attempt to combat smartphone-distraction by becoming better multitaskers. We will not attain more meaning in our lives by becoming more adept at dividing our attention. Many meaningful projects, activities, and experiences, from which we are distracted by our smartphones, do not consist of tasks to be completed; they call for more dedicated, involved engagement. I believe that overcoming our current smartphone ailment calls for carving out certain occasions for more focused interaction with one's physical environment, culture, and others (one's milieu).[1]

To begin to understand such involved engagement, and to understand why it can be rewarding and meaningful, we need a conception of experience that will help us to identify what we might be missing when a significant portion of our day's experiences are punctuated by scattershot smartphone-use. If we work with an indistinct characterization experience, we will fail to understand the active-experiential aspect of meaningfulness, as well as the depth of the problem with smartphone-distraction.

Now, I do not mean that we need an accurate account of the neurophysiology of various experiences; I am not talking about identifying the brain activity that may be causally explanatory of this or that experience. I am talking about *describing* experience effectively. Attempting to correctly describe experience is at the core of the philosophical method of phenomenology. Whatever the ultimate explanatory story may be regarding brain states, or however the metaphysical issues may shake out, phenomenologists set these aside (we bracket them, we put them "out of gear"). If we can hit upon effective descriptions of the relevant experiences, this will suffice for the purposes of this book. Whatever the ultimate metaphysical accounts and scientific explanations may be, we do not dispute them; we are just not engaged in these projects. (In fact, phenomenologists will claim that we need to get the descriptions right *before* scientific investigators can do their work effectively—the descriptive enterprise is primary in at least this sense.)

I believe that John Dewey's account of experience is fruitful to consider in this context. I am interested in employing but modifying what he calls "*an* experience." I will try my best to avoid Dewey's metaphysics, focusing on the ways in which he describes experience.[2] In this chapter, we will examine his "*an* experience"; toward the end of the chapter, I will settle on a modified notion which I will call "developed experience."[3]

I want to begin by taking a brief detour to say something about why we are turning to Dewey's account of experience. A good number of standard conceptions of experience in the history of philosophy are problematic. This is, in part, due to the fact that many of these conceptions of experience emerge within epistemic theories. In other words, many prominent philosophical approaches to experience have emerged within investigations into the nature, sources, and foundations of knowledge. The problem is that these philosophically influential accounts offer narrow and wan characterizations of experience, focusing as they do on an experiential foundation for knowledge at the expense of other aspects of experience.[4] In Martin Jay's telling of the history of conceptions of experience, in his *Songs of Experience*, he attributes narrow accounts of experience to the usual figures—René Descartes, John Locke, David Hume, and Immanuel Kant.[5]

What William James calls "the psychologist's fallacy" is his critique of the metaphysics of such epistemologists' accounts of experience.[6] But the critique is also directed at the narrowness of these epistemologist-conceptions of the *character* of experience, which is in the territory of what concerns us, describing experience. While I will include a quotation of James farther below, I want to quote Thomas Alexander first, because his description of James's "psychologist's fallacy" speaks to our purposes more plainly than the original:

> In trying to account for how empiricists and idealists had cooked up such a thin and impotent account of experience, James had argued that they had merely read the discrete manipulable *results* of their analytical accounts into the primary, original state from which they had been abstracted as having been their pure, pristine shape all along. In short, they had converted the fruits of analysis into the roots of experience.[7]

Dewey agrees with James here (incidentally, so does the phenomenologist Maurice Merleau-Ponty).[8] The critique is that such analysts divide up the perceptual experience of, say, an apple into impressions such as "red" and "sweet." Next, they conclude (incorrectly) that these atomic impressions (or "ideas," "representations," or "sensations") are what the experience of an apple consists of originally, pre-reflectively. We have here the epistemologists making a metaphysical claim, and then we have James and others flagging the mistaken maneuver of assuming that the after-analysis description of experience captures the features of experience as it is prior to analysis. This critique of the epistemologists' metaphysics of experience is given support by carefully considering our experience itself. The support consists of consulting one's own experience, and discovering that one does not find such atomic impressions (and also consulting with others to confirm that this introspective finding is not idiosyncratic). This is a critique of the metaphysics of experience arrived at by carefully describing experience.[9]

To return to what is most relevant for our purposes, which is the character of experience and the thinness of the epistemologists' conceptions of this character, James makes the point that one cannot arrive at an accurate description of the character of experience by building it up out of atomic parts. James very-briefly voices this concern, and then the metaphysical critique, in the following.

> The continuous flow of the mental stream is sacrificed, and in its place an atomism, a brickbat plan of construction, is preached, for the existence of which no good introspective grounds can be brought forward, and out of which presently grow all sorts of paradoxes and contradictions, the heritage of woe of students of the mind.[10]

The experiential support for the metaphysical critique, as I mentioned above, is that "no good introspective grounds can be brought forward." That is, we do not introspect these atomic impressions. The concern about the thinness of this conception of the character of experience comes at the beginning of the passage: "the continuous flow of the mental stream is sacrificed." James's *stream* characterization is preferable to the atomized characterization. As Alexander notes, "The moment of genuine perception ... should be the beginning for any adequate theory of experience." The mistake made by the epistemologists is that they take "minimal moments of experience as paradigm," minimal moments such as "a swift act of bare identification and categorization."[11]

Examining Dewey's "*an* experience" will help us to understand the structure and elements of active, rich experiences. "[F]rom the commencement of Dewey's philosophical life," Alexander tells us, "he was concerned with developing a theory which would do justice to the fullness, richness, and organic complexity of experience. This is the underlying motive of Dewey's thought from first to last."[12]

From his perspective in the 1930s, Dewey notes his concern with the impact upon experience of the hustle and bustle of the modern world:

> Zeal for doing, lust for action, leaves many a person, especially in this hurried and impatient human environment in which we live, with experience of an almost incredible paucity, all on the surface. No one experience has a chance to complete itself because something else is entered upon so speedily. What is called experience becomes so dispersed and miscellaneous as hardly to deserve the name.[13]

In our time, one reason that many of our experiences do not "carry through to completion" has to do with our frequent interactions with our smartphones.[14] Through Dewey's clarification of what is required of us to develop experiences, we will see this flip side clearly; that is, Dewey will show us what it looks like when experiences fail to develop—when they are aborted, stunted, incomplete. Dewey's description of experiences that fall short of being *an* experience will throw smartphone-distraction and its impact into relief.

3.2 The Structure of *an* Experience

According to Dewey, *an* experience, and experiences that are not developed in this way (which we can refer to as undeveloped experiences), are different in their degree of development but not in kind. What does this mean? It means that all experiences share an underlying structure. All experiences involve more developed or less developed phases of what Dewey calls doing and undergoing (aka doing and suffering)—this includes practical experiences, intellectual experiences, and aesthetic experiences. One can have, for instance, a practical experience that is *an* experience or a practical experience that is undeveloped. Here is Dewey's description of the doing-and-undergoing structure of a simple, practical experience.

> A man does something; he lifts, let us say, a stone. In consequence he undergoes, suffers, something: the weight, strain, texture of the surface of the thing lifted. The properties thus undergone determine further doing. The stone is too heavy or too angular, not solid enough; or else the properties undergone show it is fit for the use for which it is intended. The process continues until

a mutual adaptation of the self and the object emerges and that particular experience comes to a close.[15]

Contrasting practical activity with intellectual activity, Dewey writes: "The creature operating may be a thinker in his study and the environment with which he interacts may consist of ideas instead of a stone."[16]

Failures of what we might call awareness (what Dewey calls perception) prevent a given experience from developing. We need to consider what it means to perceive or to be aware of the various phases of any given experience. But first, I imagine a reader wondering why "experience" does not refer only to the undergoing phase. This is a natural question but it is important for us to sort out what is incorrect about it. Dewey contends that the doing, undergoing, as well as the perceived relations between these phases are requisite aspects of *an* experience. I want to interpret this to mean, simply, that our acts (our doings) must be perceived (we must be aware of them), as must the relations between doings and undergoings.[17] One point we are extracting from Dewey here is that *an* experience is not passive. A straightforwardly passive experience is one in which we are only aware of what we undergo. In order for a given experience to develop, one must ensure that one's actions are accompanied by awareness, and one must also become aware of the relations among phases. *An* experience is active in this sense. If I do not take the initiative to perceive what I do, and to perceive what happens, and the way in which what I do is related to what happens, as well as the relations between the various happenings, then my experience cannot develop. "Experience" refers to all of these aspects. (Recall, from Chapter 1, that the distinction between passive experience and active experience will become important in relation to meaningfulness.) This has been abstract; below, I will explore this structure of experience, as well as other features of *an* experience, through examples.

Keep in mind that we are on the lookout for a way of understanding smartphone-distraction. Note the relevance of what we have said so far to distraction generally. Whatever the distraction may be, when we are only half paying attention to our situation we do not perceive every instance of doing and undergoing.[18] Here is an example. In the early 1980s I was a cashier and cook at Pizza Hut. One night—this was unusual—a customer paid with a $100 bill. I accurately counted his change. I then gave him his change ... *and* the $100 bill! He stood there, in front of me, looking directly at me stone-faced (imagine Buster Keaton) waiting for me to realize what I had done.

What happened here? I was aware of (I perceived) some of what I was undergoing (I recognized that I was given a $100 bill), and I perceived some of what I was doing (I counted out the correct change). But I was not paying attention to everything I did; I did not consciously note the fact that I gave Buster the $100 bill and the change. Personifying the mindless cashier, I wasn't even perceiving all of my actions, my doings, let alone the relations between them. I was distracted. In this case, there is a *practical* problem: "The properties thus undergone" did not "determine further doing."

3.3 Relations Between Doing and Undergoing

In any experience, when we do perceive every instance of doing and undergoing the experience becomes more developed. But even in such a case, we may be missing the relations, which are essential building blocks of a developed, unified experience, *an* experience.[19] One's awareness of the relations seems to be the glue that makes a given experience flow from one part to the next. According to Dewey, in *an* experience, "flow is from something to something. As one part leads into another . . . [it] carries on what went before."[20]

As we have already seen, Dewey is concerned that our experiences are too often disjointed. In the following quotation, he explains what we fail to do that results in experiences being undeveloped.

> [I]n much of our experience we are not concerned with the connection of one incident with what went before and what comes after. There is no interest that controls attentive rejection or selection of what shall be organized into the developing experience. Things happen, but they are neither definitely included nor decisively excluded; we drift. We yield according to external pressure, or evade and compromise. There are beginnings and cessations, but no genuine initiations and concludings. One thing replaces another, but does not absorb it and carry it on. There is experience, but so slack and discursive that it is not *an* experience.[21]

Too often, in passive experience, we fail to become aware of the ways in which the phases of a given experience are joined; we miss the relations altogether. Another failure is not to be sufficiently engaged in the experience, which leads to awareness of only certain relations. Either of these shortcomings prevent experiences from developing. A phase of experience should take up aspects of previous phases; the phases should be related, and we should be aware of this. In addition, we will see that there is often interpretive work to do in actively perceiving relations.

Note that smartphone-distraction is one kind of yielding "according to external pressure." We have here a new way of understanding smartphone-distraction: smartphone-distraction is not merely a problem insofar as it interferes with the effective completion of tasks (as it was conceived in the social-science studies considered in Chapter 2); *smartphone-distraction can disrupt the development of experiences.*

Consider this example of *an* experience that has a certain quality that would not have emerged if the experience had been cut off. In music, general qualities depend upon a listener's perceptions of the relations among individual qualities. I am thinking of general, harmonic qualities such as dissonance or melodic qualities such as anticipation. There are also rhythm examples. Individual, minute, rhythmic oddities, timing nuances, which may be individually felt as tensions can add up, when repeated, to constitute more general qualitative features of a performance or a recording. Consider the general quality of the buoyancy of a rhythmic groove. As I put it in *Groove*, "For listeners as well as players, the buoyancy of a groove is the result of the felt support that comes from finding equilibrium in repetition, even if it [the equilibrium] is built upon . . . [rhythmic] pulls and pushes. Even a groove that has a disjointed feel repeats, and when it does, we grow accustomed to it. As we get used to it, the feel becomes uplifting and invigorating."[22] The pertinent point here is that if one does not have an uninterrupted experience of the music—if one is distracted by a smartphone notification (say)—the broader quality of buoyancy will simply not emerge in experience. We could make a similar point about harmonic and melodic qualities in music that develop over several measures.

To obtain a clearer sense of the importance of the relations between doing and undergoing, consider a sort of unnatural situation in which some relations are missing altogether from the situation itself, so they could not be perceived even if one tried. The following example will make the role of relations stand out. To be clear, what I have in mind is not merely a case in which the relations are there but one is not attending to them; rather, I am imagining a situation in which some material that could possibly become relations between doing and undergoing is missing in the situation itself. This will be a case in which the experience continues but there is a lack of continuity among the parts due to missing relations; it is a disjointed, undeveloped experience.

One consequence of the sickening Trump presidency is that many of us in the United States have watched more television news than is psychologically healthy. If you, like me, are in this group, then you are familiar with the following mediocre type of cable news television host. Imagine a segment the host is leading in which he has a "conversation" with three guest political pundits. This host has questions prepared in advance, which he reads from a teleprompter. As a result of conducting the segment in this manner, the host's second and third questions do not take into consideration answers to previous questions. And there are no impromptu, substantive follow-up questions. The parts of this conversation are related in the mere sense that answer-follows-question and question-follows-answer. But the details of the questions and answers are not woven together by the host, as they typically would be by the participants of an actual conversation.

Now, the host cannot have *an* experience of the segment because some key relations between doing and undergoing—viz., between the content of questions and answers—are literally missing. In fact, since these relations between doing and undergoing are missing in the situation itself, the guests and television viewers will also not have *an* experience (unless they are having *an* experience that brings-in other content, such as the contemplation of the strangeness of a host asking questions but repeatedly not listening to the answers).

The salience of the relations between doing and undergoing is not merely practical, as it appears in Dewey's stone example ("properties thus undergone determine further doing"). As we have been considering, being aware of these relations is necessary for the development of any given experience. Dewey warns: "experience is limited by all the causes which interfere with *perception of the relations* between undergoing and doing."[23] Being consciously aware of the relations means not only to perceive the fact of the connection, and not only to perceive that which connects a given doing to an undergoing (the connecting tissue could be, e.g., to notice that something asked by one person in a conversation is addressed in a response by another). Being aware of the relations means to perceive, in addition, what one does and undergoes *as joined*. For example, in a conversation, if one person's question and another person's answer suggest agreement, then *noting that agreement* is to perceive the joined doing-and-undergoing.

Early in *Art as Experience*, leading up to the examination of the relations between doing and undergoing which we have been considering, Dewey approaches the general notion of the relations between phases of experience from a very broad perspective, in terms of how one experiences one's own past, present, and future as related. In order to incorporate Dewey's discussion about the past, present, and future into our consideration of experience's phases, and relations between phases, we need to take the past, present, and future to be very broad phases of experience themselves. Dewey observes, "Most mortals are conscious that a split often occurs between their present living and their past and future."[24] But it turns out that Dewey is referring to a phenomenon worse than merely a split. It is not merely the case that the past and future tend to have no effect on the present; the past and future typically have a negative effect on the present. The past is too-often experienced in the present as a burden. "[T]he past … invades the present with a sense of regret, of opportunities not used, and of consequences we wish undone. It rests upon the present as an oppression."[25] And too often, the future shows up in present experience as ominous: "we exist in apprehensions of what the future may bring."[26]

The preferred way of living, according to Dewey, is to adopt one's past, to allow the past to inform the present: "the live creature … can make friends with even its stupidities, using them as warnings that increase present wariness."[27] Similarly, regarding the future, Dewey encourages us to experience the future not apprehensively but as consisting of possibilities. "Only when the past ceases to trouble and anticipations of the future are not perturbing is a being wholly united with his environment and therefore fully alive."[28] "Fully alive," here, is a reference to vitality, generally speaking, but it is also a reference to developed, unified experience, *an* experience. Past and future are not just related to the present temporally; there are important relations between the past, present, and future that we must be aware of if we are to have an integrated life. What Dewey is describing is not only the *perception* of relations between past, present, and future; he is encouraging us to *interpret* previous and future phases of experience in a certain way, and to utilize these interpretations in a way that is conducive to well-being. This is a further sense in which experience can be considered active.

One reason I expanded the scope of our consideration of the structure of experience just above is to note that the stakes of distraction increase as we consider experience in a broader sense. For example, in the moment when one is doing the mental work of "making friends" with a past error, a distraction from a smartphone notification that sidetracks one from this interpretive work can be devastating for one's general well-being.

3.4 Job Interview Example

Experiences of many sorts can become *an* experience. In Steven Fesmire's *Dewey*, he mentions a set of examples that speak to the range of experiences at issue: "writing a book, buying a house, going on a date, making a snowman, or running a double-blind experiment."[29] I want to look closely at one of Dewey's ostensibly mundane examples, a job interview, in order to explore additional features of *an* experience. Here is one aspect of his description of the job interview:

> Two men meet; one is the applicant for a position, while the other has the disposition of the matter in his hands. The interview may be mechanical, consisting of set questions, the replies to which perfunctorily settle the matter. There is no experience in which the two men meet, nothing that is not a repetition, by way of acceptance or dismissal, of something which has happened a score of times. The situation is disposed of as if it were an exercise in bookkeeping.[30]

Dewey's point is that if the interview is conducted in this mechanical way, *an* experience is not in the offing. As described, this interview is somewhat like the cable news segment above: the interviewer is asking prepared questions; the interviewee is providing stock answers. Without really thinking about the questions, the interviewee is simply identifying into which category a given question fits so that he can provide a pre-prepared answer for questions of that kind. (Recall that I mentioned this sort of recognitional experience in Chapter 1.) Dewey criticizes this sort of merely recognitional or identificational perception insofar as it arrests experience before it has a chance to develop. As he explains:

> In recognition we fall back, as upon a stereotype, upon some previously formed scheme. Some detail or arrangement of details serves as cue for bare identification. … In recognition there is a beginning of an act of perception. But this beginning is not allowed to serve the development of a full perception of the thing recognized. It is arrested at the point where it will serve some *other* purpose, as we recognize a man on the street in order to greet or to avoid him, not so as to see him for the sake of seeing what is there.[31]

In order to foster the development of any given experience one's perceptual engagement must be active. Recognitional experiences are minimally active for a limited duration. For Dewey, this is related to his emphasis that one must perceive doings, undergoings, and relations. Note the subtlety of Dewey's description of active experience in the following quotation, where experiential activity is characterized metaphorically as plunging-in, answering, and pitching.

> Perception is an act of the going-out of energy in order to receive, not a withholding of energy. To steep ourselves in a

subject-matter we have first to plunge into it. When we are only passive to a scene, it overwhelms us and, for lack of answering activity, we do not perceive that which bears us down. We must summon energy and pitch it at a responsive key in order to *take* in.[32]

As we have seen, grasping the relations between doings and undergoings is to grasp continuities or discontinuities, to grasp experiences as unified. To return to the job interview, as described above, the interviewer is not engaging with the answers sufficiently to allow the answers to generate adjusted questions, nor is he asking follow-ups. The experience is stunted because both parties are participating on a near-passive automatic pilot.

However, Dewey believes that *an* experience could emerge even in a job interview. Imagine that both parties attend to the particularities of the questions and answers, engaging in an organic conversation about the issues at hand. Both parties attend to each other's questions and statements as well as to how each question or statement lands with the other, introspectively and empathetically. Further, imagine that both parties perceive the ways in which these elements are related, the ways in which these questions and statements "clash or fit together," as Dewey says.[33] Perceiving the doings, undergoings, and relations, will establish continuity in the experience, possibly leading to *an* experience of the interview. If a job interview transpired in the rich way I just described, it would stand out among job-interview experiences; it may even stand out among experiences in general. In order to get a better sense of why this is the case we need to consider Dewey's notions of *consummation* and *pervasive quality*, which are features of *an* experience.

3.5 Consummation

We can see, even in the simple example of the man picking up a stone, that Dewey finds the sources of *an* experience as "rooted deep in the world itself"[34]—more specifically, rooted in an individual's engagement with her environment. Consider this statement: "The outline of the common pattern [doing-and-undergoing] is set by the fact that every experience is the result of interaction between a live creature and some aspect of the world in which he lives."[35]

This means that we can seek to understand *an* experience by examining our most basic engagement with the world. When we look to this engagement we find not only doing and undergoing, but also the experiential phase of *equilibrium*. An individual falls out of practical balance with his environment in terms of thirst (say), and then takes action to recover balance, equilibrium, by finding and drinking water. Attaining such equilibrium is a positive experience. As Dewey observes:

> Every need, say hunger for fresh air or food, is a lack that denotes at least a temporary absence of adequate adjustment with surroundings. But it is also a demand, a reaching out into the environment to make good the lack and to restore adjustment by building at least a temporary equilibrium. Life itself consists of phases in which the organism falls out of step with the march of surrounding things and then recovers unison with it.[36]

Reaching equilibrium with one's environment is, first, to experience a lack, to act, and then to be practically satisfied. This practical structure can help us to understand *an* experience—even experiences that are not practical (recall that *an* experience might be practical, intellectual, or aesthetic). We have already considered the doing and undergoing aspect of the structure of *an* experience, with an emphasis on the relations. The present aspect of the structure of experience that I want to consider is that even *an* experience that is not practical involves something like a phase of experiential equilibrium, a special sense of experiential completion that Dewey calls consummation.

Think back to the job interview example of *an* experience. Notice that if the outcome of the interview is that the interviewee is hired, then he achieves practical equilibrium regarding employment.[37] Although this has the structure we are looking for, this is not the kind of case we are interested in, because the resulting satisfaction here can be understood to rest on satisfying practical needs or desires. We want to consider experience more generally, including but not limited to the practical.

What about the case in which the interviewee is not hired? Surprising though it may seem, this can be *an* experience. I want to consider the claim that such an experience can be consummatory. How so? If the experience is developed, it mirrors the structure of a more basic, practical experience that is *an* experience. The basic source of the satisfaction is in the structure of seeing something through to the end, but this satisfaction is colored, qualitatively, by the various tensions resolved in the phases of the experience. The coloring, so to speak, of the satisfaction is one way in which the culminating phase of *an* experience is integrated with other phases of the experience. Each occurrence of overcoming some resistance or tension does not merely restore the equilibrium of some previous state; it enriches it, it enriches it qualitatively. This quality is present in the phases, and it colors the completion, which just is a consummation. Consider, again, Dewey's description of very basic experience.

> Life itself consists of phases in which the organism falls out of step with the march of surrounding things and then recovers unison [equilibrium] with it—either through effort or by some happy chance. And, in a growing life, the recovery is never mere return to a prior state, for *it is enriched by the state of disparity and resistance through which it has successfully passed.*[38]

Now, in the case of the job interview, the discussion consists of a give-and-take, where, ideally, both parties are attentive to the relations between questions and answers. Perhaps the interview consists of the kind of verbal jousting present in a challenging and invigorating exchange, where mutual respect is displayed, even though the conclusion turns out to be *practically* unsatisfying (the interviewee is not hired). And the interview does not end abruptly; it reaches a natural completion, a consummation. What is this consummation? It is something like an *experiential*—rather than practical—equilibrium or completion, a satisfaction. The interviewee had something at stake, practically, which heightened the mood. Imagine that the interviewer respected the way the interviewee was putting himself on the line, even though the interviewer concluded that the interviewee was not a good fit for the available position. In this sort of case, the interviewee (and the interviewer) may look back and take note of the fact that this job interview stood out from others—and perhaps even stood out from other conversations. Even though he didn't get the job, we can imagine the interviewee looking back and thinking, as Dewey says, "that *was* an experience."

As I have suggested, when Dewey refers to "consummation," he is not referring to the conclusion of simple acts such picking up a stone, even where this involves doing, undergoing, and awareness of the relations. He has in mind more complex cases that involve multiple phases of doing and undergoing, and which typically involve resistance or perhaps even adversity. As he says,

> Between the poles of aimlessness and mechanical efficiency, there lie those courses of action in which through successive deeds there runs a sense of growing meaning conserved and accumulating toward an end that is felt as accomplishment of a process.[39]

Dewey directly addresses the complexity of consummation in an earlier book:

> Words such as *climax, peak, culmination*, refer to consummatory objects. Any object or event that can be called by such names has an intrinsic reference to what went before. The words indicate that what preceded did not merely occur before the time of the peak but that they were such as to have the climacteric outcome as their own issue.... A man may take a drink of water almost automatically to quench thirst. If he is journeying in a barren land and forms an estimate of where he may find water and upon going to the spot quenches his thirst, he has a heightened quality of experience. Water is appreciated as he does not appreciate it when all he has to do is to turn a faucet and hold a tumbler under the stream that flows out. His experience has the representative quality of being an eventuation, a consummation.[40]

To interpret this conservatively, the pertinent point is that the consummation of the experience, a satisfying completion, has one qualitative character or another, which has accumulated within, and has been shaped through, the various phases of the experience. Here is one of Dewey's direct characterizations of *an* experience.

> [W]e have *an* experience when the material experienced runs its course to fulfillment. . . . A piece of work is finished in a way that is satisfactory; a problem receives its solution; a game is played through; a situation, whether that of eating a meal, playing a game of chess, carrying on a conversation, writing a book, or taking part in a political campaign, is so rounded out that its close is a consummation and not a cessation. Such an experience is a whole and carries with it its own individualizing quality and self-sufficiency. It is *an* experience.[41]

An experience—through which one enjoys a sense of consummation—is completed; it is not interrupted. If we are having an engaging conversation but are interrupted before we finish, or if we just abruptly break it off, then the experience is not developed. (In the previous quotation, Dewey also mentions that *an* experience possesses an "individualizing quality"; we will consider this issue in the next section.)

Dewey offers the following examples of *an* experience.

> It may have been something of tremendous importance—a quarrel with one who was once an intimate, a catastrophe finally averted by a hair's breadth. Or it may have been something that in comparison was slight—and which perhaps because of its very slightness illustrates all the better what is to be an experience. There is that meal in a Paris restaurant of which one says "that *was* an experience." It stands out as an enduring memorial of what

food may be. Then there is that storm one went through in crossing the Atlantic—the storm that seemed in its fury, as it was experienced, to sum up in itself all that a storm can be, complete in itself, standing out because marked out from what went before and what came after.[42]

The example of the storm is interesting. Notice that the consummation pertaining to the storm-experience is not due to the positive, practical outcome that one has survived; it is *an* experience because of the completeness of the experience of the storm, and one can imagine various tensions experienced. This example, as well as the initial example of a quarrel, show that *an* experience is not valued owing to a preponderance of pleasure (Dewey also raises the example of being sick with the grippe as *an* experience).[43] This point is emphasized by Alexander: "Such experiences may not always be of a world or of a creature who is happy, pleasant, or at harmony."[44] An argument that ends a friendship could, and often is, cut off abruptly, where the experience seems to lack closure. The friendship ends but with unresolved questions, ambiguity, and some confusion. Imagine another kind of case in which there is still a quarrel that ends a friendship but the discussion runs to completion. One has a sense of closure. Even though this is a very negative experience practically speaking, we can imagine it being more satisfying than the previous kind of abrupt end to a friendship.

Here is an interesting passage from Alexander in which he makes some insightful comments about consummation, as well as a critique of Dewey's word-choice:

'The consummatory' was, perhaps, a homely term even for Dewey. It is meant to connote that the experience consummates the ideal possibilities of experience. There is an immanent sense of accomplishment in *an* experience, though that sense may be one of tragic resolution. There is, even so, the awareness of a process brought to fulfillment.[45]

Regarding "fulfillment," in the above quotation (and elsewhere), Alexander seems to be using the term as a synonym for "consummation." In some places, Dewey seems to do the same,[46] Perhaps Dewey occasionally uses "fulfillment" and "consummation" with different meanings. If so, in such cases he may take "consummation" to be a special kind of completion, which stands out in comparison even to fulfillment. (Given this term's importance for us in sorting out connections to Susan Wolf, I will discuss "fulfillment" further in Chapter 4.) I disagree with Alexander's critique of Dewey's word choice, because I believe that the resonance between "consummation" and "orgasm" highlights for us that one feature making *an* experience special is that it is, we might say, a supremely completed experience—"*so rounded out* that its close is a consummation and not a cessation."[47] Dewey's use of "consummation" indicates that *an* experience ends with a completion that is especially satisfying.

3.6 Pervasive Quality

An experience is unified. *An* experience is, as Richard Bernstein characterizes it, "one that is marked off from the rest of our experience by its wholeness, integrity, and unity."[48] Dewey believes that we all have a rough sense of what *an* experience is. As a provisional way of identifying *an* experience, Dewey reminds us that some experiences stand out in our memory. We remember them as standing out from our many daily, undeveloped experiences. He says: "Experience in this vital sense is defined by those situations and episodes that we spontaneously refer to as being 'real experiences'; those things of which we say in recalling them, 'that *was* an experience'."[49]

It is *an* experience's pervasive quality that marks its unity.[50] As Alexander explains, "The unity of a plurality of events or interactions mark it out as an affair or 'event' … In conscious experience, this unity is qualitatively apprehended in a prereflective manner."[51] This means that we grasp the unity by having a sense of its distinctive character, but not through conceptual analysis or rational reflection. As John Stuhr makes the point, a pervasive quality is "the defining mark" of *an* experience.[52]

But what does it mean for a given experience, as a whole, to possess a quality? We typically conceive of qualities as features of individual things (or perhaps as features of experiences of individual things). An apple is *sweet*, a rock is *hard*. Dewey's claim is that pervasive qualities, such as "distressing, perplexing, cheerful, disconsolate, … permeate and color *all* the objects and events that are involved in an experience."[53] Dewey offers an elaboration through examples of artworks:

> A painting is said to have quality, or a particular painting to have a Titian or Rembrandt quality. The word thus used most certainly does not refer to any particular line, color or part of the painting. It is something that affects and modifies all the constituents of the picture and all of their relations.[54]

It is fitting that Dewey mentions art, because the qualitative aspect of *an* experience just is aesthetic.[55] For Dewey, aesthetic qualities are not merely qualities of artworks or qualities of experiences of artworks; *an* experience of all kinds has an aesthetic quality. Dewey puts it this way:

> *[A]n* experience of thinking has its own esthetic quality. It differs from those experiences that are acknowledged to be esthetic, but only in its materials. The material of the fine arts consists of qualities; that of experience having [an] intellectual conclusion are signs or symbols having no intrinsic quality of their own, but standing for things that may in another experience be qualitatively experienced.[56]

In other words, although only certain instances of *an* experience are aesthetic experiences, all pervasive qualities are aesthetic. As Bernstein makes plain, "Pervasive quality is aesthetic quality. Anything which is distinctively *an* experience ... has aesthetic quality."[57] But what, exactly, is the difference between aesthetic experience and other kinds of experience? In addition to trafficking in different materials (as Dewey mentions in the quotation above, the materials of aesthetic experience are qualities), in aesthetic experiences, as Alexander helpfully clarifies, qualities are rendered explicit.

> Throughout the development of *an* experience, there is the pervasive sense of the regulating but nondiscursive quality which provides the context of meaning in the situation. While this quality remains tacit in ordinary experience, it is explicitly felt in aesthetic experience.[58]

Relatedly, Alexander points out that the aesthetic is a particular way of "articulating" experience.[59]

Consider again the cable news example. There are rare cases in which a particularly good host *will* ask follow-up questions based on an interesting comment just made by a guest pundit. The discussion will take an interesting and surprising turn, and then the host may ask the next guest to expand upon the point, or occasionally one pundit will jump in to ask another pundit a follow-up question. In these rare cases, a real, engaging conversation develops. This real conversation may be developed enough to possess a noteworthy quality in the pundit's experience, or the host's, or in a viewer's experience. Perhaps such a pervasive quality could be described as lively and surprising.

A reader may wonder—May we use two words to describe a single pervasive quality? Yes. Dewey maintains that pervasive qualities are ineffable. A pervasive quality, as he says, "is not anything that can be expressed in words for it is something that must be *had*."[60] In fact, Dewey holds that each instance of *an* experience has a *unique* pervasive quality.[61] If pervasive qualities are unique and ineffable, then the terms used to refer to them are only rough characterizations, and it stands to reason that one ought to use descriptive language to attempt to capture a quality in words to whatever extent is possible, including phrases and longer descriptions.

There is an interesting distinction that gained some traction in the philosophy of art in the 1960s that is helpful here; it centers on the concepts of direct and indirect description.[62] Direct description is essentially naming; indirect description involves characterizing the circumstances and context in which a feeling is experienced. While direct description—describing a perceived quality with a word—typically falls short of adequately characterizing subtle qualities, indirect description can often be more effective. You can see where I am going here; I want to make the point that it is natural and effective to describe a pervasive quality by means of an indirect description. Further, I want to make the point that there is nothing controversial about experiencing subtle, holistic qualities.

W. E. Kennick borrows the distinction between direct and indirect description from Ludwig Wittgenstein, who, in *The Brown Book*, considers the feeling/experience of familiarity.[63] Wittgenstein points out that there are different experiences of familiarity. He claims that in order to correctly describe a particular experience of familiarity, we must describe the circumstances or context.

> Different experiences of familiarity: a) Someone enters my room, I haven't seen him for a long time, and didn't expect him. I look at him, say or feel "Oh, it's you"—Why did I in giving this example say that I hadn't seen the man for a long time? Wasn't I setting out to describe experiences of familiarity? And whatever the experience was I alluded to, couldn't I have had it even if I had seen the man half an hour ago? I mean, I gave the circumstances of recognizing the man as a means to the end of describing the precise situation of the recognition.[64]

Following this passage, Wittgenstein refers to a direct description of a table (giving the shape, dimensions, and so forth); he then notes that an indirect description of the table might be the kind of description one finds in a novel: "'It was a small rickety table decorated in Moorish style, the sort that is used for smoker's requisites' . . . if the purpose of it is to bring a vivid image of the table before your mind in a flash, it might serve this purpose incomparably better than a detailed 'direct' description."[65] We can take familiarity to be a pervasive quality, and we can use Wittgenstein's observations as support for the notion that we might employ indirect description in attempts to do our best to characterize various pervasive qualities that mark this or that instance of *an* experience.

3.7 Developed/Undeveloped Experience and Smartphone-Distraction

I will not attempt to draw a fine line between developed and undeveloped experiences. It will serve our purposes to conceive of experiences as on a continuum, with developed experiences on one side, undeveloped experiences on the other. Here, then, is my modification of *an* experience as *developed experience*. Take developed experiences to be active. They are not stunted in early phases of doing and undergoing. They will not cease with early recognition. They will have at least an incipient pervasive quality, shaped by their phases (that is, there will be some qualitative glue or resonance connecting the phases). Therefore, necessarily, the experiencer will be aware of more than a few relations among phases. But, will all developed experiences have a consummation? No. It is easy to imagine some experiences that are not stunted, which are not cut off at recognition, which are satisfying indeed, but do not reach all the way to consummation. These are experiences that are satisfying but slightly disappointing in the end, given that they do not quite reach a full completion. This is not a wholly negative prospect, given that such experiences can even function as some motivation for one to return to the activity that generates them. Using the term "developed experience," rather than "*an* experience," also enables me to set aside Dewey's metaphysics, focusing on his *description* of these rich experiences, and it allows me to loosen the criteria, as above, regarding what counts as a developed experience.

The contrast, *undeveloped experience*, is straightforward. Undeveloped experiences are stunted, cut off early in the process, before or at recognition. They are passive. A pervasive quality does not take root; there is no resonant experiential quality. There is very little awareness of the relations among phases. And there is certainly no consummation.

What stands in the way of the development of any given experience? For our purposes, we want a clear picture of this obstruction, because we want to understand what it is about smartphone-use that can interfere with the development of experiences. I want to focus on two kinds of obstruction to the development of experiences which Dewey emphasizes: a lack of mental energy and interruption.

Dewey refers to a lack of mental energy as "inner lethargy," by which he means perceptual drifting or a general mental sluggishness.[66] We have seen that developed experiences require activity.[67] One cannot have a passive developed experience. If one's perceptual approach is sluggish, one will not probe and actively attend to various aspects of the situation at hand. One will likely fall short of adequately perceiving the relations between doings and undergoings. Recall that perceiving a relation is not a simple perceptual act; it often involves detecting and experientially registering qualities such as a tension or an agreement (recall the job interview example). Dewey notes the importance of this attention to relations: "Experience is limited by all the causes which interfere with perception of the relations between undergoing and doing."[68] Alexander makes this point in terms of interactivity: "*An* experience comes to be in the development of perception which takes an interactive approach to the material of experience, the world."[69]

We can detect the importance of activity in experience by noticing that perception requires interpretation to one degree or another. We might think of recognition as a very basic kind of interpretation, but recall that Dewey takes mere recognition to be a case of undeveloped experience. Recognition involves making initial sense of what one sees, for instance. This is minimally active; Dewey's concern is that once a recognition is achieved, the "valve" of activity, so to speak, is turned off. This is where the experience stops developing, as Dewey remarks, "Recognition is perception arrested before it has a chance to develop freely."[70] Above, I mentioned Dewey's example of encountering someone on the street, engaging in active experience momentarily until one recognizes the person. Once this recognition is achieved, one stops exploring the person's features (and other aspects of the situation) because one has made the recognition; one knows who it is.

Interpretation can continue, it can be more complex. To consider a specific example, the philosopher R. G. Collingwood describes the mental work that is required to make sense of what a speaker is saying during a lecture. Understanding a lecture requires more than merely registering the noises that come out of the lecturer's mouth; it requires mental effort to reconstruct the meanings intended by the speaker: The meanings are "inaccessible to a person who cannot or will not make the efforts of the right kind, however completely he hears the sounds that fill the room in which he is sitting."[71] Note that this activity is required merely to achieve a basic understanding of the lecture; cultivating a developed experience at a lecture requires even more attentiveness and interactivity.

Perceiving actively so as to explore and make sense of a situation, to give the experience a chance to develop, seems to require continual engagement, to be steeped in the situation. The kind of smartphone-distraction we are considering, such as having a text conversation, prohibits one from being steeped in the *interconnected* phases of a developing experience. Referring back to Chapter 2, we can say that engaging in the developing experience of a lecture while texting on a smartphone is an attempt at strong multitasking. It is not the viable kind of multitasking, weak multitasking, such as talking with a passenger while driving on a country road. So it is not at all surprising that strong multitasking with a smartphone will interfere with a developing experience—especially given the active, ongoing demands of cultivating a developed experience.

Commonly, we assume that if we are distracted, we can simply return to our previous area of focus to pick up where we left off. If one is engaged in serial multitasking, however, one moves in and out of a situation, engagement is intermittent. There is a lack of continuous attention. Developing experiences are just too fragile and structurally complex for this approach to be effective. This interference, or interruption, is the second sort of obstruction to a developing experience. At any time, being lured away from a perceptual act aborts a developing experience, the experience just breaks off in mid-development. Dewey's folksy way of putting this is to refer to being distracted from one's work while plowing a field; plowing, here, is a metaphor for all work, all projects: "We put our hands to the plow and turn back; we start and then we stop, not because the experience has reached the end for the sake of which it was initiated but because of extraneous interruptions or of inner lethargy."[72] In such cases, Dewey maintains that the experience will have holes, "dead centers."[73] This, then, is a feature of an undeveloped experience. Such a structural flaw in any given experience prevents it from developing into a unified whole. Due to its dead centers, the experience cannot take on a pervasive quality; there is no chance of consummation. As compared to a developed experience, an undeveloped experience is incoherent, inchoate.

We have seen that strong multitasking comes at a cost to performance. In relation to the studies we considered in Chapter 2, one cost for healthcare workers may be a mistake in administering medicine. Such examples are understandable in terms of a means and ends framework. If the nurse is involved in texting with a friend while preparing a dose of medicine, he may be pulled away from his work, and this may result in administering the wrong dose. But if the nurse can redirect his attention to his task in-time, he can make a correction, and there will be no damaging cost to performance; the event will be a "near miss." *The cost involved in being distracted from a developing experience is quite different. Once a developing experience is interrupted, it's over. There is no way to return to where one left off. The performance cost (if we want to call it that) of having a text conversation while engaging in a developing experience is to abort the experience; it's over; it's finished.* This is to drain the experience of unity, to turn it into an incoherent, undeveloped experience. *One is not able to turn away from a developing experience and then return to it a minute later; One cannot pop in and out of a developing experience.* The elements that make it the experience that it is are developing and integrated. We now have a better sense of what I said in 2.3: We cannot understand the impact of smartphone-distraction upon developed experiences through a means/ends orientation because the consummation, or the near-consummation, is not an isolable end; many of the elements of a developed experience are interdependent and intertwined.

Consider an example. We encountered empirical confirmation in the social-science research that even muted smartphones can distract a user. When you are waiting for a particular text message, a vibrating notification in your pocket can pull you away from interaction with your milieu (notice that a notification is typically a solicitation to engage in off-task activity). But even if you are not waiting for a particular text, vibrating notifications indicate that there is new information in your phone, *possibly* something interesting. During some phases of a developing experience, the mere possibilities in your phone, indicated by a notification, may be more titillating than the present phase of the developing experience. This smartphone-distraction is likely to pull you away—not even because of what it is, but because of what it *may be*. "We put our hands to the plow and turn back"; the turning-back is akin to turning one's attention to the phone.

3.8 Taking Stock

We need an account of experience that will enable us to understand rich experiences, and to understand precisely the nature and effects of distraction. We find this in Dewey's account of "*an* experience," which I interpret conservatively and refer to as developed experience (3.1, 3.7).

Practical, intellectual, and aesthetic experiences have the same structure (3.2). There are two main phases of experience, *doing* and *undergoing*. And importantly, there are relations between the phases. "Experience" refers to all of these components. Any given experience can be developed or undeveloped. In order for any given experience to develop, one must engage actively, perceptually; experiences cannot develop in passivity. This means that one must be actively aware of (perceive) one's doings, undergoings, and the relations among them (3.3).

Any distraction that interferes with one's awareness of doings, undergoings, or relations will cut off the development of any experience. Here we begin to see that smartphone-distraction is not merely a problem insofar as it interferes with the effective completion of tasks; smartphone-distraction can disrupt the development of experiences (3.3). In fact, such distraction is likely to put an end to a developing experience (3.7).

In a minimally active experience, the experience ceases to develop once a recognition or identification occurs. In a straightforwardly practical experience, this is appropriate (e.g., I can stop looking at the stoplight because I see it has turned green). But in other experiences that are potentially richer, such aborting of an experience can be a lost opportunity (see my discussion of the job interview in 3.4).

In terms of various basic needs, such as water and food, we fall out of balance with our environment, and then we recover it. Such equilibrium is a positive phase of the most basic practical experiences. Even intellectual, aesthetic, and more complex practical experiences—if they are developed—can have a completion phase that is analogous to equilibrium, which Dewey calls consummation (3.5). In a developed experience of any kind, there are multiple phases of doing and undergoing, and many relations. As we go through various phases that involve making adjustments and overcoming minor and major obstacles, an incipient character or quality of the experience emerges. The experience's consummation is the end of the experience, a completion, which possesses a finalizing quality that resonates with the character of previous stages. If a developing experience is interrupted (say, by smartphone-distraction), no consummation is in the offing.

Developed experiences are unified. Their unity is marked by a pervasive quality (such as perplexity or cheerfulness) which is the distinctive character of a developed experience (3.6). This pervasive quality is that which is incipient in various stages of a developing experience, and in its full form it makes up the qualitative character of a developed experience's consummation.

A developed experience, as I am defining it, may or may not have a consummation, but it has all of the other features of *an* experience (3.7). Undeveloped experiences lack these features: They are passive, stunted in early phases, they have no pervasive quality, and involve little or no awareness of relations.

One source of obstruction to the development of experience is inner sluggishness or passivity, which swamps the perceptual activity required for experience to develop. Perceptual activity is required for the development experience; the activity is needed for one to perceive the various phases and relations. Another source of obstruction to the development of experience is interruption. Smartphone-use—participating in a text conversation while at a small musical performance, for instance—can interrupt a developing experience (in this case, a developing musical experience).

Due to the integration of the phases and qualities in a developing experience, any kind of multitasking that involves shifting one's attention in and out of a developing experience is not feasible. One cannot engage in a developing experience intermittently. The resonances and building that occurs from phase to phase, and relations, requires continuous engagement. If one does move in and out of a developing experience, due to distraction, the experience will either be aborted altogether or it will have holes or what Dewey calls "dead centers,"[74] which will throw off the incipient qualities and hinder consummation. The latter is an undeveloped experience.

I want to highlight the two aspects of this chapter that are especially important for our larger project; not surprisingly, one has to do with meaning, the other has to do with smartphone-distraction. First, this chapter offers us a characterization of experience that is conducive to generating meaning in life. I contend that in order for an activity to be meaningful a person must have some experiences in relation to it that are not passive nor merely recognitional, in the sense described in this chapter. Some active experiences are required. The notion of a developed experience gives us a detailed account of a rich, active kind of experience that can effectively contribute to meaningfulness. In the next chapter, I will explicitly connect developed experience to meaningfulness through Wolf's subjective condition. Second, anything that disrupts our ability to foster developed experiences can hinder our ability to engage in meaningful activities. We have seen that smartphones are particularly distractive, so they present a special concern. Smartphone-use can distract us from developing experiences. Finally, it's worth noting that whatever you think of my subsequent maneuvers to connect developed experiences to Wolf's theory of meaning in life, and to Borgmann's focal practices, developed experiences themselves are valuable ingredients of our lives. We should not allow the increasing pervasiveness of smartphone-distraction to result in our having fewer and fewer developed experiences.

4

Meaning in Life

4.1 Introduction

In this short chapter, I want to set out the basics of Susan Wolf's Fitting Fulfillment theory of meaning in life. Wolf's theory is both common-sensical and influential, especially among the (analytic) philosophers who work on this topic. As Thaddeus Metz has noted, "Wolf's theory is … probably the most commonly held view … among contemporary philosophers who have thought about meaning in life."[1] Wolf's theory can serve as a linchpin for our project, as well as a bridge between our consideration of developed experiences and our consideration of Albert Borgmann's focal things and practices.

As I mentioned in the introduction, my main claim about meaning is that engaging with focal things and practices by means of developed experiences can generate meaning in one's life. Invoking developed experiences in this way enables us to understand, in detail, the potential effects of smartphone-distraction upon the creation of meaning in life. In addition to explaining the basics of Wolf's theory, in this chapter I will build support for one aspect of my main claim about meaning by establishing connections between developed experiences and Wolf's notion of subjective fulfillment.

4.2 Susan Wolf's Fitting Fulfillment Theory of Meaning in Life

Susan Wolf maintains that meaningfulness is but one dimension of a good life. A good life has three dimensions—happiness, morality, and meaning. As she reflects,

> In offering an account of meaning, I have been mainly concerned to bring out and illuminate the existence of this dimension of value in a life, distinct as it is from both happiness and morality. I have argued that there is more to life than pleasure and duty, and have sketched an account of another dimension along which a life may be better or worse.[2]

To put this in terms of reasons for acting, her point is that we undertake some actions for reasons other than our own happiness or duty. If we conceive of our lives only in terms of happiness and morality, this leaves out considerations of meaning. (As we see above, in Wolf's connecting happiness and pleasure, she characterizes happiness in terms of hedonism. According to a hedonist, one is considered happy to the extent that there is more pleasure in one's life than pain.[3])

Wolf gives us a general framework for making sense of what meaning in life is. According to Wolf, an activity will generate meaning in one's life as long as it satisfies certain subjective and objective conditions. Active and positive involvement with the activity are also necessary.[4] Is playing music meaningful? If so, it must satisfy the objective and subjective conditions. The subjective condition it must satisfy is that you must find playing music fulfilling. The objective condition it must satisfy is that playing music must have value independent of your finding it fulfilling; in Wolf's terms, it must be objectively valuable.

It will help to place onto the table some examples of potentially meaningful activities. Wolf mentions a wide range of activities and projects that could meet both conditions, and so could constitute meaning in one's life: "embracing … positive relationships with family and friends and engagement with political and social causes, … Creating art, adding to our knowledge of the world, preserving a place of natural beauty … efforts to achieve excellence or to develop one's powers—for example, as a runner, a cellist, a cabinetmaker, a pastry chef."[5] In addition to art generally, and her reference to playing certain musical instruments, she also mentions writing poetry.[6]

Regarding Wolf's *subjective* condition, what does it mean for activities to be "subjectively fulfilling"? She maintains that fulfillment is not simply pleasure. In fact, she says that fulfillment is not any "single specific qualitative feeling."[7] There are a range of positive subjective attitudes that will satisfy the subjective condition across various cases. Wolf also points out that fulfillment is "at the opposite end of the spectrum from attitudes like boredom, emptiness, and alienation."[8] So if I am actively engaged in an objectively worthwhile activity, and if I often find myself feeling bored (consider an assembly-line worker producing solar panels), then this activity does not satisfy the subjective condition; this activity does not generate meaning in my life. Wolf mentions a cluster of subjective attitudes that help us to better understand what she has in mind regarding the subjective condition: fulfillment, love, passion, being gripped by a project, or being "into" the project, and experiencing flow.[9] In the following passage, she speaks to the unavoidable variety at play:

> Rather than continue the search for a single term to name an attitude or psychological condition that any meaningful life must involve, it might be wiser, if less satisfyingly determinate, simply to acknowledge that there is a range of such attitudes and conditions, which includes love and fulfillment, and which reflects the kind of intentional, but also qualitatively positive, attachment to an object or activity that an agent must have in order for engagement with it to contribute to the meaningfulness of his life.[10]

I will return to the subjective condition in the next section, where I will also discuss developed experience.

How does Wolf clarify her *objective* condition? As with the subjective condition, she characterizes objectivity only roughly. She does not have in mind a strong sense of objectivity. Her view is not that meaningful activities must be objectively valuable in a sense that is "independent of human (or other conscious beings') needs and capacities."[11] Wolf makes this clear: "[T]he sense of objective value which, according to my view, is essential to meaningfulness in life, is a far cry from the sort of pure, subject-independent metaphysical property that Plato or G. E. Moore had in mind."[12] Moreover, comments in her 2016 article, "Meaning in Life: Meeting the Challenges," suggest that her conception of objectivity may not even rest on a neutral or impersonal perspective.[13] We can see in her 2010 book, in fact, that Wolf sets the bar for objectivity quite low:

In claiming that meaningfulness has an objective component (that certain projects and not others are fitting for fulfillment; certain objects worthy of love, and so on), I mean only to insist that something other than a radically subjective account of value must be assumed. Nonetheless, I must confess that I have no positive account of nonsubjective value with which I am satisfied.[14]

So, one might ask, what do we need in order rise above a "radically subjective" account of value? Wolf helps with this. The core of the objective condition is that the source of the value of an activity must come "from outside of oneself."[15] In other words, she wants some way of establishing that an activity is worthwhile beyond the fact that a given individual is gripped by it:

> It is in part because the range of activities that seem to qualify as fitting for fulfillment, and so as able to ground claims of meaningfulness, is so large and so varied that the words I have used to characterize this condition are so general and so vague. Perhaps the best of the expressions I have used in this connection is that which says that the project or activity must possess a value whose source comes from outside of oneself—whose value, in other words, is in part independent of one's own attitude to it.[16]

This is to say that satisfying the subjective condition is insufficient for determining what adds meaning to life. In order for a given activity to add meaning to life, it cannot be merely subjectively fulfilling; the activity must also be worthwhile. We saw above that Wolf uses the term "nonsubjective value" to convey this position; she also uses this term to capture this "maximally tolerant" notion of objective value in her 2007 piece, "The Meaning of Lives."[17] I believe that the term "worthwhile" effectively captures the indefinite sense of objectivity functioning in Wolf's objective condition.[18] And determining whether an activity is worthwhile may turn out to be somewhat straightforward; this is where Wolf lands at the end of her book:

> I am inclined to think that almost anything to which a significant number of people have shown themselves to be deeply attached over a significant length of time, has or relates to some positive value—that almost anything people *find* valuable (stably and in significant numbers), is valuable.[19]

So, the opinion of others matters—it is at least a strong clue—as to whether some activity is worthwhile. The number of others must be "significant," as must the length of time they find an activity to be worthwhile. Is the notion of *value* still doing any work here? Perhaps there is no need for an account of objective *value* here.

Even though it is indefinite, the objective condition is still doing important work in the theory of meaningfulness, because it gives us the leverage we need to distinguish between meaningful activities and those that seem intuitively not to be meaningful. For example, we can claim that playing live music or running is meaningful, while engaging in the project of hand-copying *War and Peace* or riding a roller coaster is not. A significant number of people have found playing live music and running meaningful for a significant length of time; this is not the case for the latter two projects (which may, nevertheless, be pleasant to some, and contribute to their happiness). A person may believe that a given project with which they are engaged is worthwhile though it is not, and the flip side is also true. For example, Wolf imagines Fred Astaire's father "wishing his son would quit dancing and get a real job."[20] She takes the observation that we are sometimes mistaken in this way to be uncontroversial, and she sees it as a supporting reason for the objective condition; an aspect of the value of meaningful projects comes "from outside of oneself."[21] She makes this clear:

> If we accept the idea that a person's judgment about the value of an activity can be wrong, then we accept the legitimacy of a kind of value judgment that is subject-independent. According to the conception of meaningfulness I am proposing, that sort of judgment is essential to understanding what a meaningful life is.[22]

Wolf also emphasizes the linkage between the two conditions. In order for a worthwhile activity to be meaningful to a person, engaging with it must be subjectively fulfilling for her. This is just what it means for both conditions to be required. Relatedly, what makes a project subjectively fulfilling is partly that one realizes that the work is worthwhile. As she says, "'[F]ulfillment' seems to me to include a cognitive component that requires seeing the source or object of fulfillment as being, in some independent way, good or worthwhile."[23] This is why there is some tension in believing that a person obsessed with crossword puzzles (say) would truly find doing them fulfilling; it is at least unlikely that he would find this activity fulfilling over a long period of time.[24] "To find something fulfilling," Wolf says, "is rather to find it such as to be characterizable in terms that would portray it as (objectively) good."[25] (Again, note that Wolf accepts that doing crossword puzzles, riding roller coasters, and other such activities may contribute to one's happiness; meaningfulness is just a different dimension of a good life. We will return to the perplexing example of solving crosswords in 5.7.)

Ultimately, maintaining that an activity is worthwhile simply because a significant number of people find it to be so, and for a significant length of time, seems somewhat unsatisfying and arbitrary. I believe we can use Borgmann's concepts of focal thing and focal practice to add detail and substance to the notion of worthwhileness; I take this up in Chapter 5. In the next section, I will consider whether the notion of developed experience can help us to flesh out at least a certain aspect of subjective fulfillment and active engagement.

4.3 The Subjective Condition and Developed Experiences

Let's back up and take another run at Wolf's subjective condition. The most basic way in which Wolf describes the subjective condition is that, to satisfy it, one must be *subjectively attracted* to the project or activity in question.[26] Another way she puts this is to say that one must have a "positive subjective attitude" toward an activity.[27] But I am subjectively attracted to chocolate soufflés; I have a positive subjective attitude pertaining to soufflés. I am subjectively attracted to soufflés because eating them is exceedingly pleasant. The same can be said for "[r]iding a roller coaster, meeting a movie star [or] finding a great dress on sale."[28] The problem is that eating even very good soufflés seems to fall outside the realm of meaningfulness. Soufflés more appropriately fit into the dimension of a good life captured by a hedonistic conception of happiness. Such activities are not candidates for meaningfulness.

As we have seen, in order to aim for a more suitable conception of the subjective condition, and in order to distinguish meaning from happiness subjectively, Wolf clarifies that the subjective attraction associated with meaningfulness does not center on feelings of pleasure but "feelings of fulfillment." I am subjectively attracted to eating soufflés and teaching philosophy but only the latter gives me feelings of fulfillment. Other projects and activities that seem to fit into the realm of meaning include playing a musical instrument, "keeping one's garden free of weeds, . . . writing a book, training for a triathlon, campaigning for a political candidate, caring for an ailing friend."[29] According to Wolf, one might find engaging in these kinds of activities subjectively fulfilling. As we have seen, another phrase she uses, which I think helps to distinguish the subjective condition from feelings of pleasure, is "being gripped" by a project or activity.[30]

Now, recall that my main claim about meaning is that engaging with focal things and practices by means of developed experiences can generate meaning in one's life. As I have said, I intend some support for this claim to come from connecting developed experiences and focal things/practices to Wolf's theory of meaning. As a first step, I want to make some connections between developed experiences and Wolf's subjective condition. In the introduction, I also said that one might take what I am about to do as fleshing out Wolf's subjective condition.

It will help to begin with the term "fulfillment." We encountered the term in the context of Dewey in Chapter 3. I will interpret Dewey very conservatively here, perhaps even deflationarily: By "fulfillment," Dewey refers only to the *completion* of a developed experience.[31] This is not what Wolf means by "fulfillment." Enjoying a completed, developed experience is not to be fulfilled in Wolf's sense. After all, Dewey claims that one can have a developed experience of an illness or the end of a friendship, experiences which do not seem to be candidates for meaningfulness. Dewey himself says that while some developed experiences center on events that are of "tremendous importance," others center on events that, in comparison, may seem "slight."[32] In drawing this distinction sharply, I am leaning on the linkage between Wolf's subjective and objective conditions; recall the point above that part of what makes an activity subjectively fulfilling is that one recognizes it to be worthwhile.

I want to claim that where we find people subjectively fulfilled by projects we do not find them having only passive experiences. Minimally active, recognitional experiences are also insufficient. Isn't active experiential engagement contained within the notion of being gripped by an activity? And to the point that fulfilled experiences do not end with recognition—how can one be gripped by an activity if all or most of one's experiences with it are stunted? I offer developed experience, then, as a characterization of experience in order to offer one possible picture, one possible fleshing-out, of what is happening when one is gripped by an activity. When one is gripped, fulfilled, experiences are sustained and developing. Moreover, it seems that many fulfilling engagements share other characteristics of developed experience. Isn't it the case that many instances of subjective fulfillment involve unified experiences? Unified experiences are certainly gratifying, subjectively attractive. One way in which experiences can be unified is qualitatively. Perhaps some subjectively fulfilling experiences are incipiently qualitative in early stages, and perhaps some reach a satisfying completion that is something like Dewey's consummation. I will continue making this case below. (In 5.6, I will similarly link developed experiences with what Borgmann calls *engagement*.)

Here is an example that brings out the connection I want to press between developed experience and subjective fulfillment. Whichever activity or project one finds subjectively fulfilling, there will be more fulfilling and less fulfilling days. Perhaps good days are days within which one engages with one's project through developed experiences, and bad days are days in which one's experiences with the project do not develop. Consider the example of running.[33] Avid runners find running meaningful. In the next chapter, we will consider what Borgmann calls focal practices; running is a focal practice. Two of Borgmann's commentators, David Strong and Eric Higgs, raise the issue of a runner's good and bad days.

> A six-mile run along Rattlesnake Creek can be boring or a mere relentless chore. Although mind, body, and world may not be quite as dissociated as in a health club, runners do feel this discord and find themselves to be out of touch at such times. Presumably, runners would not be runners were it not for better days. On the good days, runners come away … invigorated, knowing that "this is where I want to be and what I want to be doing".[34]

Being dissociated, experiencing discord, or being out of touch with various aspects of running are ways one might describe an undeveloped experience. Perhaps, on these bad days, one is not able to appreciate one's physical connection to the surroundings because preoccupation with life's pressures is intruding upon the running experience. If all of one's running days were peppered with such distractions, which stunt one's experiences, running would not be subjectively fulfilling. It is difficult to imagine that one would be passionate about a project if all or most of one's experiences with the project are stunted, undeveloped in this way.

Further, if we can take Wolf's *activity* requirement as dovetailing with the subjective condition, then this contention is even more convincing, because we see that *active engagement* in a project is essential, and this emphasis on activity resonates with the notion of developed experience. By adding that one's relationship to a given project must be active, Wolf means to rule out a passive relation to the project, as she writes:

> Finally, this conception of meaning specifies that the relationship between the subject and the object of her attraction must be an active one. The condition that says that meaning involves engaging with the (worthy) object of love in a positive way is meant to make clear that mere passive recognition and a positive attitude toward an object's or activity's value is not sufficient for a meaningful life. One must be able to be in some sort of relationship with the valuable object of one's attention—to create it, protect it, promote it, honor it, or more generally, to actively affirm it in some way or other.[35]

The detail provided in the notion of developed experience provides leverage for understanding the active-experiential mechanisms of being gripped by an activity. We can examine the doings, undergoings, relations, and evolving character or quality of a developed experience in order to make sense of what it is that piques and holds one's interest. And in this way, we can also better understand what might be missing, or what might go wrong, when one is not gripped in this way.

Consider a music example, which I take to resonate with the comments above about a runner's good and bad days. One aspect of playing drums that might grip a person comes from the structure of the relevant developed experiences. If you abort a solo practice-session abruptly, just after encountering a challenging technical problem with your playing that you cannot quickly overcome, then this practice session will not be satisfying. Repeated undeveloped experiences like this will result in your being turned off by the project of drumming. But if you stick with a practice session until you at least partially overcome the difficulty, the now-developed experience will be gratifying. Through ups and downs, doings and undergoings, challenges are overcome that generate complex and rich experiential qualities, and consummations, which pique and hold the drummer's interest. (I will return to this example in 5.5.)

Now we can take a key step forward in our understanding of the way in which smartphone-distraction can interfere with the creation of meaning in one's life. We have seen the ways in which smartphone-use may interfere with developed experiences (3.7). If this interference with a developed experience occurs in relation to a project that is potentially meaningful, the interference may chip away at a person's passion for the project. In other words, the smartphone-distraction may undercut the degree to which one is subjectively attracted to the project, which is to interfere with one's subjective fulfillment. We can imagine the drummer or runner in the above examples being too-frequently distracted by smartphone notifications. Or consider the example of a weekly dinner with friends. If one's experiences during the conversational part of the dinner are stunted, interrupted by receiving and sending texts (say), then one's experiences remain undeveloped, and one does not become gripped by the activity. The potentially meaningful activity never actually becomes so.

In the next chapter, by examining Borgmann's focal things and practices, we will learn more about the nature of some projects and activities that are potentially meaningful, projects with which we engage through developed experiences. We will attempt to flesh out what it might mean for a project's value to be independent of a given subject's attitude toward the project. That is, we will attempt to say more about what it means for a potentially meaningful project or activity to be worthwhile. In addition, we will be able to learn more about the ways in which smartphone-distraction can interfere with potentially meaningful projects.

5

Focal Things and Practices

5.1. Introduction

Some examples of what Albert Borgmann calls focal practices include a dinner with friends or family (a practice he calls "the culture of the table"), hiking, running, gardening, carpentry, attending a baseball game with friends, and playing music. In Chapter 1, I suggested that there are a range of projects and activities that many of us recognize as being potentially meaningful in some sense; as I said, I had Borgmann's focal practices in mind. I also said that more clarity is needed regarding what makes these activities meaningful. Examining Borgmann's concepts of focal practice and focal thing, and making connections to Wolf, will help us to better understand these kinds of activities and why they are potentially meaningful.[1] Borgmann offers us a way of interpreting Wolf's objective condition: Through Borgmann, we can understand *why* people consider such activities to be worthwhile, in Wolf's sense. Through Borgmann, we see that this worthwhileness is independent of a given individual, it is nonsubjective, as Wolf requires.

I also pointed out in Chapter 1 that many of us realize smartphones can distract us from such activities. What we are looking for is a better understanding of the mechanisms and effects of this distraction. In previous chapters, I have drawn connections between developed experience and Wolf's subjective condition in order to demonstrate the ways in which smartphone-distraction can interfere with potentially meaningful activities. In this chapter, I take this further by exploring connections between what Borgmann calls *engagement* with focal things/practices and developed experiences. (Recall that my main claim about meaning is that engaging with focal things and practices by means of developed experiences can generate meaning in one's life.) In a book about smartphone-distraction, the reader may wonder why I am considering focal practices such as running and hiking. One reason for considering these focal practices is that Borgmann and his interpreters' writing about these practices is helpful for understanding focal things and practices generally. But in addition, we will see that smartphone notifications (to say nothing of smartwatch-notifications) bring technological distraction directly into running, hiking, fly-fishing, and other seemingly insulated activities.

5.2 Focal Things

Focal things anchor focal practices. What is a focal thing? Let's begin with a few examples. The reader may be surprised by the sweep of examples of focal things offered by Borgmann: a meal, the wilderness, the path of a run (e.g., an ocean road), a hearth (an old stove or a fireplace), a trout, a musical instrument. To name a few of the associated focal practices, *the culture of the table* is the focal practice anchored by the meal; *running* is the focal practice anchored by the path of the run; *hiking* is the focal practice anchored by the wilderness; *fly-fishing* is the focal practice anchored by the trout (in later work, Borgmann takes the relevant focal thing to be the fishing rod). Borgmann does not develop the example of a musical instrument as he does others. What is the associated practice anchored by musical instruments? In Borgmann and his commentators, it is unclear. In order to offer a general description of focal things and practices, it will help to work with descriptions of concrete examples. Although I will consider many examples, as a side venture I will focus on the example of music, taking musical instruments to be focal things. I will claim that *musical performance* is a focal practice.

Borgmann does not rigorously define focal things, but drawing from his writing, and from the interpretations of select commentators, I believe we can say that focal things have five characteristic features: 1. Focal things have no functional equivalents. 2. Focal things connect a context. 3. Focal things make demands on us. 4. Focal things are inconspicuous. 5. Focal things are unprocurable. One reason I am offering characteristic features rather than attempting to define focal things with more precision (say, in terms of necessary and sufficient conditions) is that it is ultimately not possible to sharply separate focal things from focal practices. As Borgmann notes, "things and practices are tightly and variously interwoven."[2]

5.2.1 Focal Things Have No Functional Equivalents

What does it mean to say that a focal thing has no functional equivalent? Answering this question will be easier if we first describe what Borgmann calls a *technological device*; this concept is central to his theory of technology, which he calls The Device Paradigm. Let's say that you have the habit of making music with a guitar, a focal thing. There are, of course, other ways you might obtain music. You might access recorded music by means of a turntable, through a smartphone app like Spotify or Apple Music, or by means of a CD player. A turntable is a technological device. A smartphone app and a CD player are also technological devices, and these two are functional equivalents (at least in the sense that they are both means for obtaining digitized music). The app and the CD player are both means to an end, music. Devices make few demands on us; in fact, they disburden us. Often, devices work by the push of a button. Note the contrast: Playing a musical instrument, a focal thing, requires skill and effort (we will return to this in 5.2.3). Borgmann identifies additional features of devices: Devices disengage us from various contexts and from other people. The machinery of devices (their inner workings) are more or less hidden. Regarding the relationship between focal things and devices, Borgmann writes, "the full significance of a [focal] thing is reduced to one function which is then secured as a commodity on the basis of some machinery."[3] A fireplace, for instance, is reduced to warmth which is delivered by a furnace or a space heater (devices).

As we will see, focal things are quite different from devices. A guitar is not merely a means for procuring music. If it were, we could straightforwardly grasp how a guitar could have a functional equivalent. But if a guitar is valuable in other ways as well, then identifying a functional equivalent becomes more problematic. The primary complexity is that a guitar is deeply integrated into its context. Given this, we cannot seek to understand it nor its value by employing a division between means and ends; such a division would be artificial and misleading. We cannot understand a guitar without understanding its integration into its context. And we cannot understand the value of a guitar without understanding this contextual integration. A guitar is not replaceable by a bass guitar, of course. And by describing its contextual effects and other features, we can make the case that even one kind of electric guitar (say, a Fender Stratocaster) is not functionally equivalent to another (say, a Fender Telecaster). Perhaps we can even make the case that a particular Telecaster is not a functional equivalent of a different Telecaster, due to its sound qualities, specific intonation, the responsiveness of certain strings on certain parts of the neck, its sustain, and so on.

As Borgmann remarks, "Discourse that is appropriate to [focal] things must in its crucial occurrences abandon the means-ends distinction.[4] It must be open to and guided by the fullness of the focal thing in its world."[5] (Borgmann is using "world" in the Heideggerian sense, to refer to a context of involvement.[6]) Regarding this "fullness" of a focal thing, Borgmann maintains that "nearly every discernible property is significant and an essential tie to the world of the thing."[7] We will begin to elaborate upon this rich contextuality of focal things when we consider their second feature.

In sum, what a focal thing is, and what its value amounts to, cannot be cashed-out in terms of an end, where the focal thing is a mere means. If this were possible, then one could swap out a given instrument with another that performs the same function. In this case, a musical instrument would have a functional equivalent. But since, regarding an instrument, "nearly every discernible property is significant," swapping it out would replace the focal thing with another object that has only some of the same value and aspects. Later, we will look at detailed examples that bring out this feature.

5.2.2 Focal Things Connect a Context

Focal things are not isolable things; a focal thing cannot be described adequately, nor its value assessed, in a context-independent manner. As Strong and Higgs explain, "A focal thing . . . exists as a material center in a complicated network of human relationships and relationships to its natural and cultural setting."[8] What is more, focal things gather-together, connect, various aspects of a context; in fact, as I said above, a focal thing serves as a material anchor of a context. Regarding an old stove, Borgmann writes, "a stove used to furnish more than mere warmth. It was a *focus*, a hearth, a place that gathered the work and leisure of a family and gave the house a center."[9] (Borgmann is leveraging the resonance of "*focus*," in Latin, which is standardly translated as "hearth.") The reference to warmth is important, because what practically replaces old stoves and fireplaces, as we just saw, are furnaces or space heaters, technological devices that provide only warmth.

Consider a meal, which anchors the focal practice Borgmann calls "the culture of the table" (I have been referring to this practice more colloquially as a *family dinner* or a *dinner with friends*). One reason the meal has significance is that family members or friends gather around it. The family or guests are grateful to the person, or persons, who prepared the food. Perhaps someone or a few people shopped for the food earlier in the day. Perhaps some of the food was grown in the cook's garden, another person brought wine or a dessert. These elements are connected through the meal. Some of the family or guests stay after the dinner is finished to help clean up and talk. In fact, an important aspect of this focal practice, anchored by the meal, is that it gathers, sponsors, conversation among the family and friends; as Borgmann emphasizes, "much of the meal's deeper context is socially and conversationally mediated."[10] We begin to see the centrality of sociality in Borgmann's account of focal things and practices through the examples of the meal and hearth.

Like a meal or a hearth, we cannot make sense of a musical instrument by characterizing it as an isolable thing. One reason characterizing a musical instrument as a focal thing is fruitful is that it is an effective way to articulate and underscore its capacity to draw-together other elements of its world. As a material center of the focal practice of musical performance, a guitar connects musicians and an audience, including connecting the particular guitarist to other musicians and to the audience. The guitar also connects the guitarist to physically and temporally distant aspects of the context, such as performance traditions and musicians of the past. For instance, if I am a rockabilly guitarist interested in the kind of finger-picking in which one's thumb plays a bass line, I may find myself trying to position my right hand on my instrument like Chet Atkins. My engagement with my instrument connects me to such guitarists. This connecting work is multidirectional: A focal thing, Borgmann remarks, "gathers the relations of its context and radiates into its surroundings and informs them."[11]

Notice that a technological device that provides music is not similarly integrated into its context; Borgmann claims, in fact, that devices tend to disengage us from contexts.[12] "[D]evices typically obviate and even repel engagement," he asserts. "Their commodities invite unencumbered consumption; unencumbered by, among other burdens, the demands of other people."[13] In this quotation,

Borgmann walks right up to the line of saying that technological devices are anti-social. One of his points here is that by making a commodity (say, recorded music) readily available, we are disburdened of having to learn guitar and of having to engage with others to procure music. As devices become more and more advanced, their ease of use renders various kinds of engagement unnecessary.

Regarding some of Borgmann's examples of focal things, it is straightforward to grasp how the focal thing connects us to others and to various elements of the context. But how does a focal thing such as a running-path connect us to others and to a context? David Strong and Eric Higgs meet this challenge; the following also speaks to the ways in which devices disengage us from certain contexts (note that the device corresponding to the running-path is a treadmill and perhaps an elliptical machine):

> Unlike exercise in front of a video in the controlled environment of a health club, runners experience a telling *continuity* between their focal thing, say the Rattlesnake Creek path, and the weather overhead, between the high, roily waters of the creek, the month of May, the receding snowfields, and the previous winter's snowfall. The office window from which one sees the mountains still capped with snow, the home where one lives, and the conversations one has with other members of the community are of one piece with this focal thing. The hour spent in the club exercising in front of a video . . . is *discontinuous* with this larger context of one's life, community, and place. While the function of a device captures one or a few aspects of the original thing, such as the exercise of muscles, devices sever most other relationships.[14]

Through this running-path example, we can see how a musical instrument might connect a musician engaged in the focal practice of musical performance to a place and a community even beyond a performance space. Perhaps the performance space is located in one's own community; perhaps word of the performance spreads into one's community, which initiates conversations with others. Someone who heard later about your performance from a friend mentions it to you while you are out for a walk.

Recall that, according to Wolf, a meaningful activity is fulfilling and worthwhile. In unpacking the latter (her objective condition), she says this means that the activity must have value that is independent of oneself. I take her point to be that the activity must have value that is not reducible to one's finding it fulfilling. This drawing-together, gathering, or connecting of a context, which a focal thing accomplishes, is a building block of worthwhileness. Let's say that you find playing guitar subjectively fulfilling in Wolf's sense. We can now say that guitars are worthwhile, in Wolf's sense, independently of you, partly due to their ability to connect a context in the rich way described above.

5.2.3 Focal Things Make Demands On Us

Focal things require patience, attention, and skill. A hillside running-path, for example, requires the runner not only to be in good physical condition but also to be skilled in managing the particular features of the path of the run. A fireplace traditionally requires finding, chopping, and gathering suitable wood, as well as knowing how to light and maintain a fire. Musical instruments require skillful engagement in playing; musicians and listeners also employ active listening skills. Engaging with an instrument skillfully enables musicians to play more responsively and to perceive more subtly.[15] In contrast, one of the defining features of technological devices is that, as technology progresses, devices make fewer and fewer demands on us;[16] it is easier to operate Spotify than it is to operate a stereo system with a turntable.

In order to unpack the relevant issues about skill, I want to consider the analogy between musicians and carpenters. Borgmann introduced philosophers to a rich book, *The Wheelwright's Shop*, written in 1923 by George Sturt.[17] Sturt describes running a workshop in the late 1800s that made farm wagons, ploughs, water barrels, and so on, for local farmers, brewers, millers, and others. Although this is unclear in Borgmann's writing, I will take the wood with which the carpenter works to be the focal thing.[18] I will work up to an analogy between carpenters and musicians, which will enable me to make the case that skillful engagement improves one's perceptual acuity. Here is a passage in which Sturt makes just this point.

> I have known old-fashioned workmen refuse to use likely-looking timber because they held it to be unfit for the job.
>
> And they knew. The skilled workman was the final judge. Under the plane (it is little used now) or under the axe (it is all but obsolete) timber disclosed qualities hardly to be found otherwise. My own eyes know because my own hands have felt, but I cannot teach an outsider, the difference between ash that is "tough as whipcord," and ash that is "frow as a carrot," or "doaty," or "biscuity." In oak, in beech, these differences are equally plain, yet only to those who have been initiated by practical work. These know how "green timber" (that is, timber with some sap left in it, imperfectly "seasoned") does not look like properly

dried timber, after planing. With axe or chisel or draw-shave they learn to distinguish between the heart of a plank and the "sap." And again, after years of attention, but nohow else, timber-users can tell what "shakes" are good and what bad.[19]

The carpenter's tools extend her abilities. We should think of this, I am suggesting, as the carpenter acquiring skill in her hands, which is extended by the capacities of her tools. As the carpenter *embodies* a tool, as she comes to use it seamlessly as an extension of herself, her tools become integrated into her bodily capacities (integrated into what Merleau-Ponty calls the body schema).[20] The main point here is that the carpenter's skill in working with tools helps her to grasp qualities in the wood that she otherwise would miss. In their discussion of this passage in Sturt, Hubert Dreyfus and Sean Kelly emphasize that the perceptual acuity that is fostered through skill is not merely one of fine discrimination of *visible properties* in the wood: "Rather, it is seeing immediately how the wood will respond to an axe or saw or plane, seeing immediately how it will bear up or collapse under the weight of a carriage."[21] In other words, the carpenter's enhanced perceptual acuity is directed to the work product, which is what is important in the broader context.

Similarly, a guitarist develops skill in her hands. Consider guitar picks, drumsticks, bows, and reeds to be analogous to the carpenter's tools. The musician's skills and tools are brought to bear on the focal thing, the guitar. And as the carpenter's work product is a carriage or a cabinet, the musician's work product is the music made. The guitarist's skill enables her to discern different sound qualities in different kinds of guitars which an unskilled player would miss (e.g., the difference between Telecasters and

Stratocasters, or between Telecasters made at different times or in different countries). Following Dreyfus and Kelly, I do not mean the way in which a perceptual psychologist can discern subtle properties of acoustic events; I am referring to *musical* qualities. For example, a skilled guitarist might recognize that notes played high on the neck of a particular Telecaster have extraordinary sustain, and notes played in the middle of the neck have unusual warmth.

A concern raised by these observations is that making music with pre-loaded guitar loops through music software such as GarageBand may not develop a musician's perceptual abilities as does developing the skill to use the focal thing, the guitar. Borgmann makes the general point in this way: "Physical engagement is not simply physical contact but the experience of the world through the manifold sensibility of the body. That sensibility is sharpened and strengthened in skill. Skill is intensive and refined world engagement."[22] Dreyfus and Kelly express this point succinctly: "Learning a skill is learning to see the world differently."[23] They also make illustrative observations about sports (American football and basketball): "the successful running back has 'great vision', the point guard has extraordinary 'court sense'. In each case this means that the person's skill at . . . running or passing allows them to see meaningful distinctions that others without their skill cannot."[24]

The focal thing in the focal practice of fly-fishing is the trout in his 1984 book, but Borgmann changes it to the fishing rod in his 1992 book (without explanation).[25] What follows is a 1984 description of the requisite skill involved in fly-fishing, which mostly centers on the use of the rod, and serves as a useful description of skill in using a focal thing.

There are more intricate bodily skills in casting a line that involves not just the pushing of buttons and the movement of a stick but the harmonious interplay of rod, line, and fly, compensating for the wind, avoiding the willows, using hand, arm, and shoulder while maintaining one's stance in a slippery streambed. And to have a line and finally the fly settle gently on the river, as gently nearly as a real insect might, is one of the most delicate maneuvers humans are capable of.[26]

Listening to music is itself a skill to be honed; this is true for musicians as well as audience members, and it is true regarding recorded music as well as live music. I will contend below that listening skills can be improved through the sociality of musical performance. Note that even simply watching musicians can help guide an audience member as to which sounds deserve special attention. This can often be read off musicians' movements and the visible attention musicians give to certain instruments at certain moments. A listener lacks this access when obtaining music via Spotify. We will return to this notion of engagement, in this full sense, near the end of the chapter.

Before leaving this section, it is worth noting that learning a skill seems to make one increasingly attracted to a focal thing and practice. Skill, like attention and patience, fosters engagement. This is another sense in which devices breed disengagement. (Notice, also, that *attraction* to a focal thing and practice is related to Wolf's subjective fulfillment.)

5.2.4 Focal Things are Inconspicuous

Borgmann's account of focal things is inspired by Heidegger's later writing on things and art.[27] One way in which Borgmann's focal things are inconspicuous is in contrast to Heidegger's examples of great artworks, such as a Greek temple, which could serve as a culture's orienting force, and which Borgmann considers a focal thing of a pretechnological age.[28] The Greek temple is a cultural paradigm that generates an understanding of being, as Heidegger would put it. Focal things, unlike the temple, "flourish at the margins of public attention."[29] According to Borgmann (and later Heidegger), in our technological age, great works of art like the temple have lost their ability to orient our lives; they have lost their "focusing power."[30] Like Heidegger, Borgmann believes that "we must uncover the simplicity of things";[31] thus, we look to inconspicuous things such as Heidegger's jug, Borgmann's meals, running-paths, and musical instruments. These issues are related to the claim that focal things and practices can center one's life, which we will consider later.

Given that focal things are inconspicuous, they must be brought out, activated, in order for their orienting power to work on us and to work on a context. This happens when we engage with the demands of a focal thing. A running-path is all but invisible until a runner reveals its significance by drawing upon her endurance and skills through engaging with the path.[32] Regarding a musical instrument, Strong and Higgs write, "A fine violin . . . is brought to life in the hands of a caring and gifted performer."[33] Being "brought to life," here, is to be rendered conspicuous. One may also take an historical perspective on being rendered conspicuous. An electric guitar, after Chuck Berry's "Maybellene," holds possibilities that one could not detect prior. And this was due to creative and skillful engagement with the guitar—and amplifier—which brought something out of the instrument that was not previously available. (Later, when we discuss "technological paraphernalia" the reader might think back to this example, especially to Chuck Berry's amplifier.)

5.2.5 Focal Things are Unprocurable

There is a trace of the unprocurability of focal things in what we have already discussed. Consider one of Borgmann's most direct descriptions of focal things:

> Still we might say this about focal things in general. They are concrete, tangible, and deep, admitting of no functional equivalents; they have a tradition, structure, and rhythm of their own. They are unprocurable and finally beyond our control. They engage us in the fullness of our capacities.[34]

I want to suggest that what makes a focal thing "unprocurable and finally beyond our control" is that it is deep in the sense that we cannot exhaust its possibilities. We cannot possess it and we cannot fully control it. No matter how expert a musician becomes with her instrument, there is always more in it to challenge her. In a very different context, Daniel Dennett makes this point by contrasting an autoharp with a violin or piano. "[A]utoharps," he explains, "[are] designed so that anyone can learn to play them, and with an easily reached plateau of skill. [V]iolins and pianos [are] instruments that indefinitely extend and challenge the powers of the individual."[35] In our context, this calls into question whether an autoharp is a focal thing. Whether it is or not may have to do with the way one plays it (Dennett seems to be imagining a very rote kind of engagement). But regarding our main point—isn't it the case that even virtuosos are occasionally surprised by something new that their musical instrument has to offer? (Cf. 6.3). One source of this depth are the possibilities a focal thing acquires from its context. For example, I suggest that a drum *kit* is a focal thing (I mean the drum "set," which typically includes a snare drum, kick drum, cymbals, hi-hat, tom-tom(s), and floor-tom). Different spaces, different acoustics, affect the way drums sound, which opens up possibilities of tuning and striking drums differently. Even more significantly, playing with different musicians is a rich source of new possibilities. If we can characterize the plainer focal things as unprocurable (consider a fireplace or a running-path), we will need to lean on contextual possibilities in this way.

5.3 Focal Practices

It will be helpful to begin with Charles Taylor's rough characterization of *practice*, from his *Sources of the Self*:

> By "practice," I mean something extremely vague and general: more or less any stable configuration of shared activity, whose shape is defined by a certain pattern of dos and don'ts, can be a practice for my purpose. The way we discipline our children, greet each other in the street, determine group decisions through voting in elections, and exchange things through markets are all practices.[36]

We might say that a practice consists of normed procedures, and when these norms are more explicit we might think of them as standardized procedures.

In subsequent sections, we will consider what makes a practice focal. Before turning to this, however, it will be helpful to say a few words about the focal practice associated with musical instruments. When Borgmann refers to musical instruments as focal things, he is not specific about what the associated focal practice is. The closest he comes is to gesture at musical practice broadly construed—"a long tradition of a craft, of a method, and of a musical literature."[37] More thought-provoking is a brief comment he makes in his book's opening salvo. And this earlier thought better echoes the *conviviality* of certain other focal practices he discusses later in his book, such as the culture of the table and the practice centered on the fireplace. Here is Borgmann on page 3, having just referred to a "stereo set" (turntable, amplifier, and speakers) as a technological device. In what follows, he is simply making the point that, in addition to the means of a turntable, music can be procured through musical instruments: "After all, a group of friends who gather with their instruments to delight me on my birthday provide music."[38] Musical practice broadly construed is amorphous, abstract, and in a sense, everywhere. Borgmann's standard examples of focal practices are concrete in the sense that they are practices to which one can go and in which one can engage—a hike, a family meal, fly-fishing, running. All of these practices emphasize active and concrete engagement with others and/or with the environment. It is in this spirit that I want to suggest we take *musical performance* to be a focal practice associated with musical instruments. Musical performance is a practice nested within musical practice broadly construed. I will not attempt to define musical performance since it takes so many different forms in different genres and historical periods, but I have in mind live music played on musical instruments for physically-present listeners, performances that involve at least one musician (although I tend to consider interactions among groups of performing musicians).

5.3.1 Focal Practices Safeguard Focal Things

In order for a practice to be *focal* in Borgmann's sense, the practice must safeguard a focal thing. This is the main feature of a practice that is focal. Why do focal things need safeguarding? I'll answer this from a few different perspectives. Here, first, is an answer from what we might consider a psychological perspective. Without a practice, our engagement with a focal thing is at the mercy of our one-off decisions, which turn on the precariousness of moment-to-moment shifts in inclination and motivation. It is challenging to repeatedly motivate oneself to engage in demanding activities without drawing upon the support of habit, or better and more elaborately, a practice. In Borgmann's words, a focal practice guards a focal thing "against the vicissitudes of fate and our frailty";[39] "A [focal] practice keeps faith with focal things and saves for them an opening in our lives."[40]

Let's pan out a bit. In our culture, we have a strong preference for convenience and efficiency; this puts pressure on our engagement with focal things. It is difficult to rationalize engaging with focal things on grounds of efficiency. Given this, there is a danger that, over time, we may replace most or all focal things with devices. Modern technological devices appeal to our preoccupation with efficiency by making it very easy for us to obtain goods such as food, exercise, and music. Our impatience makes it tempting to replace a family meal with what Borgmann calls "technological food" (fast food, microwavable food, etc.).[41] It is tempting to replace a run outside with treadmill-running or an elliptical-machine workout. It is tempting for a musician to replace a musical instrument with pre-loaded instrument loops on GarageBand, for a music enthusiast to replace the musical instrument she might learn to play with Spotify,[42] or for a music enthusiast to replace attending performances in-person with YouTube videos of performances (or officially streamed performances). The larger context is that one main goal of technological progress is to relieve us of burdens, to make our lives easier. This is a laudable goal, obviously. But in this cultural context, we may come to view engagement with focal things as burdensome. According to Borgmann, some interactions with things and with other people which may seem burdensome are actually opportunities for meaningful engagement. As he says, we often "fail to distinguish genuine liberation from disengagement."[43]

Heideggerians will interpret a cultural preference for convenience as ontological. According to Heidegger, in our technological age, everything shows up as a resource; in Heidegger's terminology, everything "reveals itself as standing-reserve."[44] What this comes to, according to Hubert Dreyfus, is that "the essence of modern technology … is to seek more and more flexibility and efficiency *simply for its own sake*.… our only goal is optimization."[45] If this is right, then the danger to focal things is not merely due to cultural preferences or psychological frailty; it is due to our current *understanding of being*, our cultural paradigm. In our age, efficiency has become an end in itself.[46] And we do not experience this as a mere orientation; we encounter everything as it shows up through this orientation simply as reality showing itself as it *is*.

Borgmann's reference to means/ends thinking, instrumental thinking, serves as a straightforward way to articulate the danger to focal things. Today, when faced with the decision of whether or not to engage with a focal thing, we tend to misunderstand our options through means/ends thinking. This can lead to a misunderstanding of focal things and their value. For example, it is a mistake to understand and evaluate a family meal as merely a means to an end, eating. It is a mistake to understand a run as merely a means to an end, exercise. And it is a mistake to understand a guitar as merely a means to an end, the procurement of music. If we make this mistake, we will find ourselves justifying the replacement of focal things, one by one, with devices—we will come to conceive of focal things as having functional equivalents.

In 2.3 I claimed that the studies of smartphone-distraction in healthcare and education that we considered in 2.1 and 2.2 frame what we are distracted from as tasks that can be understood in terms of means and ends. I claimed that some meaningful activities cannot be accurately understood nor assessed by being carved up into means and ends. The discussion in this section, and in 5.7, fill out this claim. We see that, for Borgmann, to think about the family dinner in terms of means and ends lays the foundation for its being replaced by a trip to the drive-through. In our case, we are focused on the fact that potential meaningfulness is to be had in the focal practice. *We want to understand effective activity within a focal practice, and then explicate where and how that activity can be interrupted by smartphone-distraction. Means/ends thinking gets us looking at the wrong phenomena; this is the shortcoming of the social-science studies for our purposes.*

Why should a new musician invest so much time learning to play guitar when she can make use of pre-loaded instrument loops on GarageBand or some other music-creation software? Aside from the perceptual acuity reasons associated with skill that we considered above, and aside from the variety in creative ideas and options that are open to a person with skills vis-à-vis a focal thing, another reason is that the value of committing herself to engagement with an instrument is not exhausted in the music she makes. Musical instruments are not mere means. (We will address this reason directly when we discuss centering in 5.5.) Consider also the case of the music enthusiast. Why learn to play piano to procure music, or why bother going to a musical performance to hear live music, when you can get all the music you want through Spotify and YouTube? As above, if the analysis of choices focuses on the end, music, the technological shortcut may appear too appealing to resist. What we are considering is what Borgmann refers to in the following passage as "the technological diremption into means and ends": "It is certainly the purpose of a focal practice to guard in its undiminished depth and identity the [focal] thing that is central to the practice, to shield it against the technological diremption into means and ends."[47]

Instrumental thinking also inclines us to mistakenly characterize certain aspects of focal practices as superfluous when they do not clearly enhance an end. To take an example pertaining to musical performance, instrumental thinking may result in conceiving of the camaraderie of making music with people you know well to be inessential and ultimately disposable. Consider a rock singer-songwriter who is deciding whether to continue performing with his current band of friends. From the instrumental perspective, it may seem expedient for him to hire "better" side musicians, "hired guns." Regarding instrumental thinking generally, Borgmann remarks, "When we look at a tree accordingly, we see so much lumber or cellulose fiber; the needles, branches, the bark, and the roots are waste. Rock is 5 percent metal and the rest is spoils. An animal is seen as a machine that produces so much meat. Whichever of its functions fails to serve that purpose is indifferent or bothersome."[48]

Let me drive home what we have said so far about guarding, and make the connection to Wolf's objective condition. This sense of preserving or guarding a focal thing by means of a practice, which we have just been considering, is different from the psychological sense of guarding in which one's individual motivation needs to be propped up by a practice. The former sense of guarding has to do with staving off the conception of focal things as means. Focal practices preserve our ability to understand focal things as *worthy* of our investment in-themselves, not as mere means. My contention is that focal things are worthwhile in the sense required by Wolf's theory of meaningfulness. A guitar is valuable not merely because I am "into" it—not merely because I find it subjectively fulfilling, in Wolf's sense. Within the focal practice of musical performance, a guitar is considered to have value independently of a particular person's interest in it. Later, when we consider focal things and practices together, we will return to this point.

Before closing this subsection with some examples, we should unspool the thread of instrumental thinking all the way to commodification. The instrumental approach, means/ends thinking, in which one fails to value focal things themselves, and fails to value the participation in a focal practice itself, and instead approaches a thing as a means to an end, can lead to commodification. Commerce encourages, and is fueled by, instrumental thinking. Commerce encourages us to conceive of the value of focal things and practices in terms of an end product; the end product is what might become a commodity. The more we conceive of music as a commodity, the more this end-product is valued, and the less we value the associated musical instruments and performances as focal things and practices. When we devalue the focal practice, we also lose the rich contextuality of the live music itself. Below, while making this point about commodification, Lawrence Haworth is offering cooking and filmmaking as focal practices.

Devices are not the only threats to focal practices. Any change that leads people to engage in their practices for entirely instrumental reasons . . . is a threat. A cook or film director who lacks integrity, that is, who does not cook or direct with an eye to doing the work well but instead is entirely motivated by a desire to sell or to please, finds all of the goods associated with cooking or filmmaking to be external to those practices.[49]

By *external goods*, here, I take Haworth to be referring to exchange value, pleasure brought about by the end-product, social-media "likes," and so on. He continues: "In that case the practices are not focal and they have no internal goods."[50] (Focal things are *internal goods.*) Conceiving of musical performance as a focal practice aids us in keeping our evaluative focus where it should be; it helps us to avoid conceiving of the engagement with musical instruments as a mere means to produce a product that one sells. Interestingly, if one does conceive of making music, films, or cooking in these external-goods terms, these activities would fall into the dimension of a good life Wolf calls happiness, not meaningfulness (cf. 4.2). This provides some reassurance that connecting focal things and practices to meaningfulness is in-line with the spirit of Wolf's intentions. Applying Wolf's distinction here between happiness and meaning also brings out the importance of preserving focal things through practices in the arts and other such pursuits.

An example of musical performance can help us to better understand the import of a context established by a focal practice as well as the context-dependence of relevant features. I have been making the point that we should not take focal things to be mere means, and that focal practices guard focal things against such instrumentalism. In the previous section, I made a related point:

Making sense of a focal thing—what it does, as well as its value—cannot be explicated in a one-dimensional manner in terms of a singular end. Recall Borgmann's statement about focal things: "nearly every discernible property is significant and an essential tie to the world of the thing."[51] Musical performance, a focal practice, is a context in which the multi-dimensional contextually-dependent significance of musical instruments can emerge. This is to say that one way in which musical performance guards or preserves musical instruments is that performance provides the very context that is a condition for the possibility of the multi-layered character and significance of musical instruments.

The context-dependence at issue is relevant not only to musical instruments but also to the music performed. Performing musicians make choices that are informed and shaped by a specific performance context. And the musical qualities that emerge make the most sense within that specific context. A tempo, for instance, which a band may agree is perfect at the time—for this night, during this part of the set, when the audience is in this mood, at this venue—may sound too slow or too fast at a rehearsal, on a recording, on another night, or earlier on the same night. Many performing musicians have had the experience of listening to recordings of live performances, lamenting a seemingly too-fast or too-slow tempo. My suggestion is that a recording of a song that sounds too fast or too slow (or a groove that seems to push too hard or seems to lean too far backward) may not have actually been too fast or too slow during the performance. The way the tempo or groove sounds *during the performance* is the decisive standard. A good drummer tracks this live energy, is immersed in it, or even guides it, and she builds the energy into her counting-off of songs and her playing. This is one problem with determining a tempo in advance and playing to a click track. This brings to mind some sad concert videos of The Who's drummer, Keith Moon, with earphones duct-taped to his head, trying to play live to an obviously-too-slow click track, which probably seemed to be the perfect tempo at a rehearsal. Strong and Higgs speak to this kind of particularity regarding the focal practice of running: "The sights and sounds, the events of the run, the uniqueness of a particular run, or the harmony one feels with the surroundings cannot be instantly replayed at our disposal."[52] These contextual phenomena—the fact that this tempo sounds right or wrong at this show—are made possible, guarded, and preserved by a focal practice.

We can probe this example further. This contextual dependence enables us to draw some interesting distinctions between live music and recorded music. Some aspects of musical instruments, and a musician's relationship to them, are not captured in recordings. And in some cases, this is directly relevant to the music. Consider the drummer Clem Burke in his early Blondie days. Burke's tom-tom (which is mounted on the bass drum) was not tilted toward him for easy striking, as is common; instead, it was pointed directly up. Striking it required more effort than is usual; sometimes he would literally raise his body off his throne to strike the tom-tom. In live performance, his tom-tom fills may sound more or less identical to the way they sound on a recording. But seeing him make the unusual effort for every tom-tom strike and fill has a visceral effect which is available only in the seeing. This seeing adds to the emphasis and energy of a tom-tom strike or fill. The fact that Burke occasionally incorporates tom-toms into his repeating rhythms makes some of his live grooves more energetic and urgent as experienced live as opposed to what shows up on a recording, even a live recording (I am thinking of the introduction and verses of "Dreaming"). Seeing this performed live on video is one thing; being physically present for a live performance implicates an audience-member in this energetic, bodily investment, the mood of the venue, and the actions and movements of other audience members—these all contribute to the particular sense of energy and urgency one encounters in the live music. The focal practice of musical performance establishes and preserves this context. (For whatever it's worth, my bet is that Burke pointed his tom-tom north not just for looks, but because he wanted to "work for it"—he liked, I'll bet, what this physical difficulty did to his choices and playing style.)

A focal practice can guard multiple focal things, and it can even guard aspects of the practice that are not focal things, as we have seen (including what I call in 5.4 "technological paraphernalia"). As Haworth makes plain, a focal practice "secures everything involved in its significance; it brings depth to the tools and other 'means' by which the point of the practice is achieved."[53] Note that even a venue—a place—can be guarded by a focal practice, as it accumulates significance through time, housing many performances. For example, First Avenue and the 7th St. Entry, the venue, may have been a dirty and smelly space at 9:00 a.m., but as a part of the focal practice of musical performance it had a unique ability to wrap a musical event in significance.

5.3.2 The Traditions, Procedures, and Standards of Focal Practices

I have been emphasizing the guarding role of focal practices, where the value of the resulting practice seems to rest on what is guarded (focal things, that which they generate, and so on). In his, "Focal Things and Focal Practices," Lawrence Haworth argues that, in addition to the inherent value of focal things, value is generated by the traditions, procedures, and standards that constitute a focal practice.[54] Haworth considers the focal practice of a Japanese tea ceremony, in which the focal thing is the tea cup. This example provides an illustrative cluster of procedures that are steeped in tradition.

> Tradition specifies that one should receive the proffered bowl of tea with the right hand and place the palm of one's left hand under the bowl; that before drinking the tea one is to turn the bowl to the left and in such a way that the most beautiful side of the bowl is turned away; that one is to sip noisily; that after sipping one is to wipe the area where the lips have touched the bowl with the thumb and forefinger of the left hand; that after eating the tea cake one is to wipe the bowl again with the napkin that accompanied the tea cake; that one is to again rotate the bowl to the left so that one may finally admire the beautiful scene on the bowl.[55]

The emphasis on procedures is helpful regarding the example of musical performance. In addition to the value of focal things, a portion of the value of musical performance as a focal practice—as well as the value of its output, live music—is due to the traditions, procedures, and standards of musical performance. Some norms are very general; for example, musicians face the audience, and the audience shows appreciation in one way or another. Some procedures are subtle; for example, in rock and jazz, in counting off a song, the count should reflect the tempo and groove. In rock music, there is a quite strange tradition regarding encores, which involves pretending that the show is over (everyone knows it is not), waiting for the audience to demand an encore, playing one encore, and then pretending, again, that the show is over (it's not). In the encore case, a narrative of the event takes shape, it is given structure, anticipation builds, and so on. These are valuable elements of musical performances (even if some seem artificial with time).

Regarding some focal practices, Haworth claims that the value of focal things themselves is ultimately due to these procedures, norms, and traditions of the practice. As he makes the point, "the excellence of focal things in some practices is constituted by the practice and its tradition."[56] Haworth raises examples of arts and crafts. Perhaps the example we considered of the wheelwright also fits into this category, where the focal thing is the wood.

It seems that musical instruments acquire most of their significance from musical practice more broadly construed (rather than musical performance). But if we take musical performance to be a practice nested within musical practice generally, then musical instruments enter the focal practice of performance as already significant things. They are preserved by the focal practice of musical performance. The point to emphasize here is that the focal things, what they generate, and other aspects of the practice acquire additional value from the procedures and norms of musical performance.

As the reader knows, I want to claim that focal things and practices are worthwhile in a sense that we can connect to Wolf's objective condition. In this context, it is interesting to note that Wolf also believes that value can be generated in this way, through the procedures, norms, and traditions of a practice. Regarding artforms such as haiku and sonnets, she writes,

> [I]nitially, I assume, these conventional forms had no value in themselves. The interests and commitments to them that poets

and poetry lovers had was not, therefore, a response to a value in these poetic forms that was already there. Rather, their value emerged *from* the interests and commitments of people who were attracted to them, or who agreed to the strictures imposed by these forms just for fun or challenge.[57]

5.3.3 The Sociality of Focal Practices

Focal practices can extend one's capabilities. As Borgmann observes, "Through a practice ... 'human powers to achieve excellence, and human conceptions of the ends and goods involved, are systematically extended."[58] To be sure, our capabilities are extended due to the procedures, norms, and simple repetitiveness of a practice. In addition, sociality within a focal practice can extend one's capabilities. Notice that some focal practices are more social than others; musical performances and festive meals are typically more social than hiking or running. We have seen that musical performance adds value to the music and to musical instruments; it can also extend the capabilities of both musicians and audience members. Musical practice generally has this capacity, and so does musical performance. A musician, while performing, can aspire to forms of musicianship, expression, and communication that will not be open to her while playing alone— and a portion of these possibilities will not be available while playing at a rehearsal with others, nor in a recording studio with others.

Performing musicians are engaged in real-time communication with other musicians and with the audience. The audience, by engaging and reacting to what the musicians do, support an interactive loop. Consider jazz musicians' conception of live improvisation as a conversation among musicians. This conversation elicits responses from the audience. The ongoing conversational loop has the potential to enhance everyone's experience, as well as the music generated. How so? Musicians can be propped up, emboldened, by the shared nature of this enterprise. In addition, an audience member's listening skills can be cultivated by the experience of engaging in the music with others.[59] Here is one kind of case pertaining to audience members. When musicians in musical conversation accomplish something noteworthy yet subtle, some less-experienced audience members may not grasp the significance. The reactions by the more-experienced audience members can draw the less-experienced audience members' attention to particular musical moments, thereby potentially improving their musical discernment. In the case of grasping grooves, being drawn in to the way others move their bodies can be a key. In *Groove*, I make the point in this way: "Finding the right kinds of movements may begin to unlock, so to speak, the key perceptual structure, which will enable you to begin to experience what you previously perceived as [merely] off-time notes, now, as pushes, pulls—a groove."[60] Like the case of tempo and other musical qualities discussed above, live grooves are specific to the particular performance; they are context-dependent. Borgmann briefly refers to the general effect of being physically present with others engaging in a focal practice as "social resonance," which, he says, generally "invigorates our concentration and acumen when we listen to music or watch a play."[61]

During the pandemic that began in 2019, we have been dramatically reminded of the general meaningfulness of sociality, through its absence. Being with others is meaningful in a very basic way. Regarding the more social of the focal practices, one way in which they are worthwhile has to do with their sociality.[62] This is a very simple point about what makes a focal practice worthwhile; there is meaning to be had in sociality (I develop this further in Chapter 6). In *All Things Shining*, Dreyfus and Kelly contend that the sociality of a sporting event can enhance its meaningfulness (recall that baseball, for example, is a focal practice):

> The sense that one is joined with one's fellow human beings in the celebration of something great reinforces the sense that what one is celebrating really is great. It is one thing to sit alone on the living room sofa and be astonished by some amazing feat of athleticism seen on the television … But moments like this take on greater meaning when they are shared with a community of like-minded folks who are experiencing the same kind of awe.… the awesomeness of the moment is reinforced when it is felt as shared by others. When it is also shared that it is shared— when you all recognize together that you are sharing in the celebration of this great thing—then the awesomeness of the moment itself bursts forth and shines.[63]

The more social of the focal practices draw from and build upon the meaningfulness of sociality; this is related to the conviviality of focal practices that I mentioned in 5.3. A musical performance is the kind of gathering in which everyone is called upon to share in something that has the potential to become meaningful for anyone involved. There is an expressive presentation of skill by performers, and there is an intellectual, creative, and perceptual demand placed upon audience members. Strong and Higgs comment upon this general value of sociality: "Communal ties can be forged when focal thing, performer, and audience come together in a performance that offers a communal celebration."[64]

5.4 Technological Paraphernalia

Let's take a step back to consider how Borgmann sees the general role of technology in our lives today. I imagine a reader who is hesitant in the face of Borgmann's view. This reader may acknowledge that musical performances, hiking, and festive dinners are meaningful, but the reader may wonder whether Borgmann is suggesting that we eliminate technology entirely from our lives. He is not.

Borgmann is not a Luddite, and he does not desire a return to the mid-nineteenth century. Perhaps surprisingly, he believes that focal things and practices can thrive in our technological society. Generally, he is appreciative of the fact that modern technology frees up our time for engaging with certain focal things and practices by relieving us of mundane burdens such as washing clothes by hand. What I want to address in this section is Borgmann's contention that certain objects of technology (but not technological devices) can be brought into focal practices—and these certain technological objects can positively augment our engagement with focal things and practices.

Borgmann draws a distinction between technological devices and technological paraphernalia. (Borgmann does not use the word "paraphernalia"; he uses the word "instruments." Here, I replace his "instruments" with "paraphernalia," even in the quotation below.)[65] Borgmann claims that technological paraphernalia—not technological devices—can positively contribute to our lives. Borgmann does not devote much space to discussing paraphernalia; his example of technological paraphernalia are hi-tech running shoes. (Recall that the path of a run is the focal thing, and running is the associated focal practice.

The devices often mentioned in relation to running are a treadmill and an elliptical machine. Running shoes are not technological devices.) Here is Borgmann:

> [T]echnology can produce *paraphernalia* as well as devices, objects that call forth engagement and allow for a more skilled and intimate contact with the world. Runners appreciate shoes that are light, firm, and shock absorbing. They allow one to move faster, farther, and more fluidly. But runners would not want to have such movement procured by a motorcycle, nor would they, on the other side, want to obtain merely the physiological benefit of such bodily movement from a treadmill.[66]

Although, as with devices, the machinery (the inner workings) of technological paraphernalia is hidden, paraphernalia do not share all of the features of devices. Importantly, while devices disengage us from focal things, practices, and other people, Borgmann contends that technological paraphernalia "call forth" engagement. He also says that technological paraphernalia "mediate engagement" with focal things and practices.[67] In their "Highway Bridges and Feasts," Hubert Dreyfus and Charles Spinosa, in reference to Borgmann, consider a dishwasher to be an example of technological paraphernalia, and they go so far as to say that it "supports" the meal, the focal thing in the focal practice of a festive dinner.[68]

Let's take a moment to explore an example of technological paraphernalia, and also to consider the ways in which this concept can be used to clarify the role of various pieces of technology within focal practices. By employing the notions of focal thing, technological device, and technological paraphernalia, we can examine the impact of various kinds of objects in focal practices (take "object" neutrally here). Recall that we are considering three different kinds of object:

(a) Some objects are *focal things*. Notice that some musical instruments, such as an electric guitar, involve quite a bit of what we might think of as modern technology. So, what makes a musical instrument a focal thing is not that it is traditional in some sense, or made by hand, but, as we have seen, that a focal thing has no functional equivalents; it connects a context; it makes demands on us; it is inconspicuous; and it is unprocurable (and as we will see in the next section, focal things have the capacity to center our lives).

(b) Some objects are *devices*. These objects have functional equivalents (they are mere means); they disengage us from contexts and other people; they do not make demands on us (they relieve our burdens); and their machinery is hidden.

(c) Some objects are *technological paraphernalia*. Unlike devices, these objects call-forth, mediate, support engagement with focal things, practices, and other people; they "allow for a more skilled and intimate contact with the world."[69] Although technological paraphernalia support this engagement, unlike focal things, technological paraphernalia do not connect a context in the sense of *establishing* connections. Examples are running shoes, and I suggest, guitar amplifiers and microphones. Unlike focal things, the inner-workings of technological paraphernalia are hidden. And perhaps paraphernalia make demands on us.

Why take a guitar amplifier to be paraphernalia rather than a device? One point to make is that amplifiers support engagement with musical instruments and musical performances, rather than disengaging us from instruments and performances (as a CD player does, for example). Guitar amplifiers make subtle sound qualities audible, which makes it possible for audience members to have more fine-grained perceptual experiences of guitar sounds. Guitar amplifiers make possible a range of guitar sounds that are not otherwise achievable, which certainly engages players. If we stretch the meaning of "thing," perhaps we can argue that the human voice is something like a focal thing. If so, the microphone certainly makes more subtle qualities of a voice available to an audience for listening (one aspect of Frank Sinatra's general innovation in singing is thought to be related to his use of the new microphone technology in the late 1930s).

If what I am saying about technological paraphernalia is correct, then what, we can ask, should be interpreted as a device in the context of a musical performance? Perhaps a drum machine, laptop, and sequencer? Although, there are probably ways of using these objects that would justify classifying them as paraphernalia—Are there uses that would result in classifying a drum machine or a laptop as a focal thing?

Even if Borgmann's concepts are not defined as rigorously as some may wish, they do provide leverage for making fruitful arguments. For example, I have suggested that a drum kit is a focal thing. Now, what can we say about replacing the snare drum with an electronic drum? Should we categorize the electronic snare as technological paraphernalia that supports engagement with the kit as a whole, and/or supports engagement with the focal practice of performance? One can argue that the electronic snare is not technological paraphernalia because it does not support engagement with the kit; it does not "call forth engagement and allow for a more skilled and intimate contact with the world."[70] In fact, one can argue that the electronic snare obstructs the drummer's engagement. Consider this reasoning. A traditional snare drum is essential to the kit's being a focal thing. Inserting an electronic snare removes central demands the kit makes on the drummer, which fosters her engagement. For example, a real snare drum sounds different in different venues, in the same venue with more or fewer people, and it sounds different with the bass guitar amplifier placed in different locations relative to the kit. Managing these differences by means of the way the drummer strikes the snare, the way she tunes the top and/or bottom snare-drum head, and through how she tightens or loosens the snares themselves, are a part of what connects her with the kit as a whole and with the performance context. An electronic snare (so the argument would go) reduces the drummer's engagement with this focal thing, the kit, and this focal practice, musical performance. It is a device.

Regarding smartphones, we have been focused on the senses in which they can distract from developed experiences and focal things/practices. But given what we have just broached about technological paraphernalia, it is interesting to consider whether it makes sense to classify smartphones as devices or as paraphernalia. It would depend upon the smartphone's use in a given context. In writing this book, I occasionally use my iPhone's Voice Memos app to record thoughts while walking. In this case, is my iPhone functioning as paraphernalia? As we have seen, when I use my Apple Music app, a case can be made that my iPhone is functioning as a device, in place of picking up a guitar. What do we say about the phone or app's *distractive* potential in either of these cases? I will return to these issues in Chapters 6 and 7.

5.5 Centering

It is fitting to consider the phenomenon of centering near the end of this chapter because it is the most general benefit to one's life of engaging with focal things and practices. According to Borgmann, the main way in which focal things and practices contribute to a good life is through centering. I am also considering centering near the end because it is unclear whether we should attribute centering to focal things, focal practices, or to both. Some of Borgmann's interpreters, such as Strong and Higgs, attribute the capacity of centering primarily to focal things, taking centering to be a feature of focal things. For example, they remark, "A thing is focal if it is what we give our time to and what we build our lives around."[71] Borgmann himself attributes the centering capacity both to things and practices. In this next passage, Borgmann attributes the capacity of centering explicitly to focal practices. (This is also his most substantive passage about music; it comes at the beginning of his book.)

A focal practice is one that can center and illuminate our lives. Music certainly has that power if it is alive as a regular and skillful engagement of body and mind and if it graces us in a full and final way. Our daily and mundane endeavors are then centered around music and invigorated by it. In such a practice the musical instrument occupies a privileged place. In many cases it embodies a long tradition of a craft, of a method, and of a musical literature. In it the melodious power of the world is gathered concretely. And it challenges humans to develop and exercise the finest bodily movements of which they are capable. In this sense a violin, for instance, is a focal thing.[72]

Relatedly, Borgmann maintains that a focal practice "is a final and dominant end which alone truly matters and fulfills and which therefore assigns all other things and activities their rank and place."[73]

To begin to get a better sense of what centering is, it is helpful to start with focal things that provide the actual, physical center of a context, such as an old stove functioning as a home's hearth. Borgmann observes: "a stove used to furnish more than mere warmth. It was a *focus*, a hearth, a place that gathered the work and leisure of a family and gave the house a center."[74] But focal things can center our lives even if they do not do so physically, even if they do not occupy a physical location that is central in our lives. It is the capacity of a focal thing to connect a context that enables it to serve as the center of one's life. But as Strong and Higgs emphasize below, merely coming into contact with a focal thing is not enough; dedicated engagement is required.

[M]ere contact with the [focal] thing, the material center, does not guarantee that this web of relations will be brought home to us automatically. A six-mile run along Rattlesnake Creek can be boring or a mere relentless chore. Although mind, body, and world may not be quite as dissociated as in a health club, runners do feel this discord and find themselves to be out of touch at such times. Presumably, runners would not be runners were it not for better days. On the good days, runners come away appreciating these *centering powers* of the thing. They come away invigorated, knowing that "this is where I want to be and what I want to be doing." Through focal things and practices they affirm the place where they live and the direction of their lives. On such days they have had a *centering experience*.[75]

In order for a focal thing to operate in this centering manner, we must give it our time and attention, dedicating ourselves to it, engaging with it skillfully and regularly. *Engagement* is the key notion here, to which we will return below.

We do not all have the luxury of dedicating ourselves to one focal thing such as a musical instrument. Even if everyone had that option, it is likely that many would not choose just one focal thing or even one focal practice. Borgmann considers the possibility of choosing two or a few focal things and practices through which to center one's life. Although it sounds paradoxical to refer to more than one center, the idea is that one can choose focal things and practices that are complementary, things and practices that resonate (which, as it were, "speak" to one another).[76] Perhaps some focal things and practices are more complementary than others. Borgmann mentions the examples of running and literature as being complementary. But what is more, "[T]here is an apparent kinship among [all] significant or focal things; and, symmetrically, there are common traits to be found among focal practices."[77] I have attempted to specify characteristic features of both focal things and practices. Given these commonalities, many groupings of focal things could be complementary to one degree or another. (My consideration of centering will continue into the next section.)

One benefit of taking musical performance to be the focal practice associated with musical instruments is that it enables me to claim that, in addition to musicians, music enthusiasts can engage in musical performances as a centering activity. A music enthusiast might select regularly attending musical performances, among a couple of other focal practices, which center her life.

5.6 Experience, Developed Experience

In the previous section, I quoted Strong and Higgs as referring to a "centering experience." They do not intend "experience" to refer merely to a mental state, and neither does Borgmann.[78] The centering phenomenon involves embodied, skillful engagement with tangible things, with the physical environment, and with other individuals. For Dewey, experience turns on concrete engagement with one's milieu as well (cf. 3.1 and 3.6). In his, "Philosophy in the Service of Things," David Strong describes an interesting give and take between individuals and focal things, which helps to emphasize that we are not referring merely to mental states:

> As people act and develop in relation to [focal] things, the things themselves are also disclosed in their manifold depth. So the potential both of what people are capable of and what things are capable of are simultaneously realized in this relation. Since both human beings and things emerge into being at the same time in this codisclosive process, and since the two require each other for this coemergence, this symmetrical relationship can be called correlational coexistence.[79]

Strong says above that "both human beings and things emerge into being at the same time." Most straightforwardly, "emerge into being" means that individuals and things become intelligible as possessing certain characteristics. On this interpretation, at least one aspect of Strong's point is that when an individual engages with a focal thing, both the individual and the thing develop, we come to understand each differently, they take on new characteristics. And as we have seen above, in focal practices, others are involved as well.

The interaction between an individual and a focal thing results in the focal thing and individual revealing characteristics of each other. The characteristics of the individual and the characteristics of the focal thing are brought out (disclosed), and then possibly altered, through interaction with the other, through skillful engagement. We can see how surprising and subtle this process can be by reminding ourselves of the unprocurability of focal things. Recall, as I asked in 5.2.5—Isn't it the case that even virtuosos are occasionally surprised by something new that their musical instrument has to offer?

As we have seen, engaging with focal things and practices can center our lives. To foreshadow our next chapter, there is something even more fundamental at stake here. We are considering a way in which a person shapes her self-identity. In the existentialist tradition, there is a belief that we *create* our selves. I just expressed this in a Nietzschean manner. Jean-Paul Sartre explores the creation of one's "essence." As Dreyfus describes Heidegger's position, a human being (*Dasein*) "takes a stand on its being."[80] Borgmann gestures at the same phenomenon but expresses the notion more straightforwardly by claiming that engagement with focal things and practices "molds the person and gives the person character."[81] Strong and Higgs point out that engagement with a focal thing develops in an individual a particular character; they put it in this way:

A fine violin, for instance, is brought to life in the hands of a caring and gifted performer, and simultaneously the life of the performer is enriched in relation to the violin. This relationship between the artifact—the violin—and the performer requires skill, and as such helps to create the character of the performer in relation to the artifact, here, the focal thing.[82]

Strong and Higgs fruitfully describe this character-creation as rising to the challenge posed by a focal thing: a "certain character . . . is developed in order to become a match for the thing."[83]

Above, I explained that when Borgmann and his interpreters refer to the centering experiences we have with focal things and practices they are not using the word "experience" to refer merely to mental states. What can we say about the kinds of experiences at issue? One move we can make is to carefully describe the interactions one has with things, others, and so on. As we saw in 5.2.3, Borgmann characterizes our interactions with focal things as involving patience, attention, and skill. For Borgmann and his interpreters, the primary way of characterizing this active comportment is to call it *engagement*. What does this mean? Borgmann explains: "the acquisition of skills, the fidelity to a daily discipline, the broadening of sensibility, the profound interaction of human beings, and the preservation and development of tradition. These traits we may bring together under the heading of engagement."[84]

Although there are aspects of what Borgmann calls engagement that are not contained in the notion of developed experience, I believe that the notion of developed experience provides a useful way of fleshing-out some aspects of engagement, which is why I have connected the two in my main claim about meaning (engaging with focal things and practices by means of developed experiences can generate meaning in one's life). We can begin, as we did in discussing the connection between developed experience and Wolf's subjective fulfillment, by noting that one cannot effectively engage with a focal thing or practice if one's experiences are passive or merely recognitional. Dewey's account helps us to understand the step-by-step process of interaction with a concrete milieu. Recall his description of the experiential phases of doing, undergoing, and the importance of one's awareness of the relations among these phases. It seems to be uncontroversial to claim that effective engagement with focal practices requires some experiences that are not cut off, aborted, or stunted. Dewey's basic emphasis on experiential completion is helpful, which is what "developed" refers to. The structure of doing and undergoing, and awareness of relations, is also helpful here in making sense of just how and where experiences are stunted or cut off, and what it means for experiences to be unified and completed.

Recall, from 5.4, Strong and Higgs's acknowledgement that a runner may have a bad day:

> [M]ere contact with the [focal] thing, the material center, does not guarantee that this web of relations will be brought home to us automatically. A six-mile run along Rattlesnake Creek can be boring or a mere relentless chore. Although mind, body, and world may not be quite as dissociated as in a health club, runners do feel this discord and find themselves to be out of touch at such times.[85]

This sort of ineffective engagement with a focal practice may turn on undeveloped experiences. Being dissociated could be explained by phases of experience being disjointed due to a lack of awareness of the relations among them. The experience is stunted. The experience is not completed. The culprit may be inner lethargy or interruption. Dewey's account not only captures an important aspect of what this engagement is, it helps us to flesh out the details of engagement, and to diagnose failures of engagement. What about Dewey's pervasive quality? We have seen that that our various interactions with a given focal thing and practice are connected to the extent that engagement with focal things and practices can center one's life. Perhaps one aspect of this connection is a unity that shows up qualitatively, as Dewey would have it, where there is a pervasive quality running throughout one's experiences with a focal practice. (Note that in order for the notion of developed experience to aid in fleshing out what Borgmann calls engagement, it is not necessary that all of these suggestions be viable and ultimately effective.)

Recall the example of a drummer engaged in a solo practice-session, which was mentioned in 4.3. Let's say that the technical problem the drummer is having is that she is struggling to play a particular rhythmic pattern smoothly. If the drummer discovers that she has a problem playing a certain rhythmic pattern, she may keep practicing until she overcomes that particular challenge. If she sees it through, then she will leave the practice session with a sense of accomplishment. Having worked through difficulties, such phases of experience will likely have a character (they are colored, they are qualitative). If this is right, as she works through the various challenging phases, this qualitative character may be recognizable as basically the same character, yet it may develop. The sense of accomplishment attached to the completion of the experience will also have a qualitative character, and I believe it is reasonable to expect that this quality will be connected to the coloring of the previous phases. What we are describing here is a consummation and a pervasive quality. Later in the day, she may find herself tapping the new pattern at various times, feeling good about her progress. In this case, the developed experience, and the pervasive quality, enriches her day even beyond the actual practice session. We are in the territory of Borgmann's phenomenon of centering. The ups and downs and ultimate consummation of the practice experience, as well as its unifying, pervasive quality, carries her through the remainder of her day, in the sense that the project of drumming enlivens her other activities. As Borgmann writes, the musician's "daily and mundane endeavors are … centered around music and invigorated by it."[86]

For our purposes, a significant benefit of connecting developed experience to the engagement with focal things and practices is that we already have a clear picture of what *un*developed experience is, through which we already have specified the negative effects of smartphone-distraction. That is, certain smartphone-use can interfere with the development of experiences (3.7). This is especially relevant to focal practices such as small musical performances, university seminars, family or festive dinners, hiking, carpentry, writing philosophy or poetry, and so on. Through these insights, we can grasp the ways in which certain smartphone-use interferes with one's engagement with focal things and practices. We can say, for example, that the reason your text conversation during a small musical performance negatively affected your engagement with the performance is that, when you began texting, you cut off your developing experience of the performance. The interconnected, qualitative thread of doings and undergoings, and their relations, was abandoned.

5.7 Focal Practices are Worthwhile

In addition to a subjective condition, we have seen that Susan Wolf's theory of meaning in life has an objective condition. The objective condition is important because it is due to this condition that we can make the case that merely being passionate about an activity (satisfying the subjective condition) does not make it meaningful. Certain activities that are merely subjectively fulfilling will *not* add meaning to one's life, such as making handwritten copies of Tolstoy's *War and Peace* or doing crossword puzzles (these are Wolf's examples).

Even though Wolf and Borgmann are working in different philosophical traditions (analytic philosophy and existential phenomenology), we can see that they are considering some of the same phenomena. Some of the activities that Wolf mentions as satisfying the objective condition mirror Borgmann's focal practices: running, creating art, music, gardening, and cooking. She also mentions cabinet-making and carpentry, which call to mind Borgmann's discussion of wheelwrights.[87]

In 4.2, we saw that, even on Wolf's own accounting, her objective condition is quite indefinite. Dating back to her 2007 article, she often uses the more open-ended term, "nonsubjective value." In 2007, another more open-ended term she employs is "positive value." And recall this statement from 2010:

> In claiming that meaningfulness has an objective component (that certain projects and not others are fitting for fulfillment; certain objects worthy of love, and so on), *I mean only to insist that something other than a radically subjective account of value must be assumed.* Nonetheless, I must confess that I have no positive account of nonsubjective value with which I am satisfied.[88]

This indefiniteness is still present in 2014. Regarding the objective condition, she rests with this cautious position: "My own inclination is to be generous in my tentative judgments about what is valuable. I expect that almost anything that a significant number of people have *taken* to be valuable over a large span of time *is* valuable."[89]

To refer to this nonsubjective value, which satisfies Wolf's objective condition, I am using the term, "worthwhile," which Wolf uses as well. It is neutral and metaphysically unencumbered. Now, first, no argument is needed to establish that the focal practices we have discussed—even those which Wolf does not mention herself—are considered to be worthwhile by a significant number of people, and have been for a significant span of time (musical performance, family and festive dinners, running, fly-fishing, hiking, gardening, carpentry, and so on). Borgmann uses different terminology; perhaps his use of the phrase "ultimately significant," regarding focal things and practices, gestures at a similar evaluative judgment.[90]

What else can we say to make the case that an activity is worthwhile? I believe we can make the case without wrestling with the metaphysics of objective value. Recall this statement by Wolf about the objective condition: "Perhaps the best of the expressions I have used in this connection is that which says that the project or activity must possess a value whose source comes from outside of oneself—whose value, in other words, is in part independent of one's own attitude to it."[91] She uses a similar phrase a few pages later—the value must be "independent of oneself."[92]

The objective condition is Wolf's way of stipulating, I believe, that meaningful activities are not worthwhile merely in an insular way; meaningfulness requires *getting outside of oneself*, establishing connections to one's milieu. *Milieu,* or *world,* in the sense of a context of involvement, implicates other people as well as many other elements of an activity's context (all of Borgmann's focal practices emphasize either a social context, a natural/environmental context, or both). Wolf refers to the notion of getting outside of oneself in an oblique way while discussing the importance of the objective condition for a theory of meaningfulness. She says that we have "a need, or at least an interest or concern, to be able to see one's life as valuable in a way that can be recognized from a point of view other than one's own."[93] The following remark, which refers to the subjective condition, emphasizes the linkage between the subjective and objective conditions, and specifically the importance of getting outside of oneself: "[T]he engagement in an activity that takes one out of oneself can be thrilling."[94]

We can see just how focal things piece together, constitute, their worthwhileness, their significance, by taking stock of how these things reach out into the world of the practice—each *reaching-out* functions like a tentacle, establishing a connection. The wheelwright established connections to his customers by building farm implements out of wood that precisely suited a farmer's particular needs. (As previously, we are taking the wood to be the focal thing.) George Sturt reflects that the wheelwright knew the needs of his particular customers, in terms of the soil of particular farmland, the curvature of particular hills on the land, and so on. In order to make effective farm implements for these particular farms, wood with certain curvatures had to be used.[95] The wheelwright was continually on the look-out for wood to fit the needs of his customers, which developed in the wheelwright a close relationship to his natural environment where he would search for wood. In this case, the wood, the focal thing in carpentry, connects the carpenter to particular customers, his community, and to nature.

These connections are not subjective; the carpenter engages with the natural environment, identifying properties of wood that are valuable for making certain farm implements. In considering Sturt's account of the wheelwright, Dreyfus and Kelly observe, "The wheelwright sees meaningful distinctions in the wood—distinctions of worth and of quality—that in no way find their source in him."[96] As I just mentioned, the wheelwright also attends to a given farmer's land. The positive value (worth) of the particular wood for making the farming implement is not merely due to the attitude of the wheelwright (whatever that would even mean). In using the implement, the farmer also values the wood's suitability for the farming implement for his land. The wheelwright's projects are worthwhile in that they connect him to the natural world and his community. His projects are worthwhile not only because he is passionate about them; his projects are valued by his customers, his community. His activities add meaning to his life.

Consider another example. Recall that a fireplace or an old stove for heating the home is a focal thing. Borgmann doesn't name the focal practice; Haworth, somewhat awkwardly, names the focal practice, "chopping wood, etc., for heating the home."[97] Borgmann's description of this practice lays out the detailed interconnections among members of the family, the thing, and nature. We can see worthwhileness taking root through these interconnections. In households in which a stove was maintained, Borgmann describes each family member as having a different, recurring task. One person chopped the wood, another carried and stored the wood, another lit the fire, and so on. The connections to nature are not merely in searching for, chopping, and carrying the wood; the seasons and time of day are marked by the skilled work and the heat of the stove:

Its coldness marked the morning, and the spreading of its warmth the beginning of the day ... It provided for the entire family a regular and bodily engagement with the rhythm of the seasons that was woven together of the threat of cold and the solace of warmth, the smell of wood smoke, the exertion of sawing and of carrying, the teaching of skills, and the fidelity to daily tasks.[98]

By connecting the members of the family to one another, and to nature, we can see how these tentacles of the practice establish shared significance, worthwhileness. There are many valuable aspects of this practice that are not due merely to one person's subjective attitude.

How do musical instruments become worthwhile? A musician comes to value her instrument through her involvement in the world of music, musical practice broadly speaking (and depending upon the musician, musical performance). Instruments matter more and more as she becomes increasingly involved. While a musician does have positive subjective attitudes pertaining to her instrument, the mattering that arises through her involvement in the world of music comes from the context, and it is shared by other musicians.

What we are seeing is that *Borgmann adds to the Wolfian approach to meaning in life by helping us to understand why certain activities are worthwhile.* We can see the worthwhileness take root in the practices.

Wolf's example of solving crossword puzzles is especially interesting because she changes her assessment of the activity at the end of her book, sort of. Early in Wolf's book, solving crosswords serves as an example of an activity that she holds to be intuitively worthless. In this early quotation, Wolf is referring to a person being subjectively fulfilled, which she characterizes, here, as being "engaged."

> Even a person who is so engaged, however, will not live a meaningful life if the objects or activities with which she is so occupied are worthless. A person who loves smoking pot all day long, or doing endless crossword puzzles, and has the luxury of being able to indulge in this without restraint does not thereby make her life meaningful.[99]

Wolf's point is that one may find solving crosswords subjectively fulfilling but it is not worthwhile (solving crosswords does not satisfy the objective condition); solving crosswords cannot add meaning to a life.[100]

However, in this later passage Wolf refers to some ways in which solving crosswords may become meaningful:

> The documentary film *Wordplay* demonstrates the remarkable range of ways in which crossword puzzles may contribute to a person's life, from those for whom it is a solitary daily ritual (and, as such, a mere harmless pleasure), to those who compete or create, to the incomparable Will Shortz, editor of the *New York Times* crossword puzzle, who graduated college with a degree in the self-devised major of enigmatology.[101]

In this quotation, Wolf mentions competition as one of the ways in which crosswords may contribute to a person's life. She intends to contrast competitive crossword-solving with the ordinary, merely pleasant, "solitary daily ritual" of solving crosswords, which only contributes to one's happiness. Competitive crossword-solving, on the other hand, can add meaning to one's life. She is referring to competition because of the annual crossword competition that drives the documentary, *Wordplay*.[102] But in fact, this annual event is not merely a competition; it is a convention, an annual meeting involving various events, although the competition is the main event, called "The American Crossword Puzzle Tournament" (spearheaded by Will Shortz).[103] In the film, crossword enthusiasts explain directly just how the annual event—the meeting and competition—adds meaning to their lives by converting solitary solving into a social activity. One solver says, "Crossword-puzzle-solving is such a solitary pursuit that when you are in a room with other people who love it the same way you do, it's like finding a lost tribe." Another attendee light-heartedly describes the meeting as "a family reunion; it's the 'screwed-up' crossword family getting together." Another mentions the "comradery" of the annual meeting.[104] In other comments, we get the sense from various solvers that their participation in the tournament makes even their day-to-day, solitary crossword activity meaningful, insofar as it connects them to the annual meeting, the competition, and their "tribe": "I'd say that crosswords, to me, are probably an obsession—certainly in the couple of months before the tournament. I kind of have this phase I seem to have worked my way into, where everything leads up to the tournament."

Now, let's assume that Wolf is correct that solving crosswords, as a "solitary daily ritual," is not meaningful; whereas, solving crosswords in a way that connects one to this annual meeting and competition is meaningful. Consider the project that involves engaging in this annual meeting and competition. Clearly, a significant number of people for a significant span of time have found this to be worthwhile (the annual meeting/tournament began in 1978). What more can we say about this project? *Why* is it worthwhile? Why have a significant number of people found it to be worthwhile for a significant span of time? This is where Borgmann can help. This crossword competition is a focal practice (call it Competitive Crossword); the crossword puzzles are focal things. Clearly, the puzzles connect the solvers to one another. The community of solvers take the puzzles and the solving activity to be worthwhile. The convention and competition get the solvers *outside of themselves*. Recall, also, that focal practices generate value through their traditions and procedures. The traditions and procedures of Competitive Crossword renders significant even one's solitary engagement with crossword puzzles throughout the year. Here are some examples of what I mean: For those engaged in this focal practice, solving-speed becomes important, even in their daily ritual (for the casual, solitary solver, speed is less important). In addition, in the tournament, points are deducted from one's score for blank squares and mistakes. So, for those engaged in this focal practice, leaving blank spaces has a significance that it does not have for the casual solver, and blank spaces have taken on this significance even in one's daily, solitary solving.

Consider a few additional features of focal things and practices to note just how these concepts help us to make sense of the worthwhileness of crosswords in the lives of those engaged in the focal practice of Competitive Crossword, as opposed to casual, solitary solvers. These focal things connect the solvers to others, and the focal things connect a context. Solving crossword puzzles requires certain skills; the competitors aim to cultivate their skills for the tournament. Note that Wolf is, in a way, disparaging the person who spends too much time engaged in solitary crossword puzzle-solving. To try to bring out the problem with such a person's interests, she compares this person to a case that seems even more worthless: "We might also consider more bizarre cases:

a man who lives to make handwritten copies of the text of *War and Peace.*"[105] I believe that Borgmann's notion of centering brings out what Wolf is getting at. It would be difficult to make the case that the life of a solitary solver is centered by crossword puzzles, but this case can be made for those engaged in the focal practice of Competitive Crossword. In the documentary, we follow some of the top solvers, and it is clear that their lives are at least partially centered by this engagement with crosswords as informed and shaped by the annual convention; those solvers who are in the top tier are quite proud of this status, in fact. Looking forward to Chapter 6, we can say that this project partially shapes their self-identity.

By working with the concepts of focal thing and practice we can clarify the difference between competitive solvers and solitary solvers. We can explain why crosswords add meaning to the life of the competitive solver. More generally, it is by dealing with examples in this way that we can flesh out what it means for an activity or project to be worthwhile. My claim, here, is that *some activities and projects are worthwhile because they center on engagement with focal things and practices.* If Wolf is right about solitary solvers, then crosswords are not focal things in this solitary context. A solitary solver is not engaged with a focal practice. The solitary-solver's activity is merely pleasant, a contribution to a good life, no doubt, but merely a contribution to the dimension Wolf calls happiness.

If we disagree with Wolf's assessment of solitary solvers, as well as other examples of purportedly worthless activities, the concepts of focal thing and practice can help. One might argue that Wolf is wrong. Solving daily crosswords does add meaning to one's life—even if one is not engaged in the focal practice of Competitive

Crossword. One might attempt to make this case by arguing that solving the daily crossword *does* connect one to others who are also solitary solvers; it connects one to the puzzle creators; it demands the cultivation of a skill, and so on. Adopting the project of counting blades of grass, on the other hand, is not meaningful because there is no engagement with a focal thing and practice. Hand-copying *War and Peace* also does not engage one with a focal practice. Recall that Wolf mentions the following activities that are pleasant but not worthwhile: "[r]iding a rollercoaster, meeting a movie star [or] finding a great dress on sale."[106] These activities do not involve engagement with a focal thing or practice.

Considering hiking and running will enable us to say more about worthwhileness. If a person is passionate about running, that passion satisfies the subjective condition for meaning in life. But in order for the activity to add meaning to one's life, the activity must also be worthwhile in the sense described above. If the worthwhileness of focal things and practices is not merely a function of a person's passion for them, where does the value of focal things and practices come from? The precise answer seems to depend upon which focal thing and practice we are asking about.[107] In the focal practice of hiking, it seems easy to make the case that engaging with the focal thing (nature, or the wilderness) is worthwhile. The thing itself is valued by others in addition to the solitary hiking enthusiast. But near the other end of the spectrum, in running, the focal thing is the path of the run. In such a case, it seems that the worthwhileness of the focal thing, and the worthwhileness of other aspects of the practice, come from the traditions, procedures, and standards of the practice (recall Haworth's Japanese tea service example and Wolf's example of haiku) (5.3.2). Running is a case in which the value of the thing and practice is generated by individuals engaging with the practice by following the procedures, aspiring to the standards, and respecting the traditions. Also note that hiking and running are worthwhile in the straightforward ways mentioned in relation to the crossword competitor: The running-path connects a context, the wilderness and the running-path engage our skills, they are unprocurable, and so on. Focal practices generally are valuable insofar as they guard focal things while simultaneously discouraging instrumental thinking in their presence. (In the concluding section of this chapter, I will elaborate upon the importance of this discouragement.)

Approaching this from another direction, Borgmann's phenomenon of centering helps us to see why engagement with a focal practice is worthwhile in the sense of providing an orientation within a person's life. That Borgmann's account is related to meaning in life is, I believe, brought home in the phenomenon of centering. A focal practice gives one's acts and experiences an interpretation, we might say, a way of understanding them as connected and significant as a result. Consider the example of musical performance. In what sense is a guitar worthwhile? We can say that a guitar attains its value from musical practice, broadly construed. Therefore, if musical performance can be taken to be a focal practice that is nested within musical practice broadly speaking, guitars and other musical instruments enter the practice of musical performance as already valuable. They are valuable independently of a particular musician's passion for the instrument and practice. The traditions, procedures, and standards generate new kinds of value within the practice, and add value to the focal things. To say that musical performance centers one's life seems very near to saying that musical performance adds meaning to one's life—and not just because one is passionate about it, but because there is something independent of oneself, pertaining to the focal practice and focal things, that is worthwhile.

The connections between Wolf and Borgmann, and between meaningfulness and centering, do not end here. Wolf allows that we might choose a couple or a few projects to give meaning to our lives, just as Borgmann allows that we might choose a couple or few focal practices to center our lives. Wolf writes, "[M]eaningfulness in life . . . [comes] from loving something (or a number of things) worthy of love, and being able to engage with it (or them) in some positive way."[108] Here is another quotation by Wolf that speaks to these connections.

> By focusing on one activity or project at a time, or on lives that are predominantly bound up with a single project, we were able to illustrate and test our ideas more clearly and more vividly than if we had discussed lives that were, or were noticed to be, more complex and varied. But most lives are more complex and varied. We have multiple roles, relationships, projects, and interests. We have families, friends, coworkers, neighbors; we belong to book clubs, church groups, bowling leagues, and neighborhood associations; we listen to music, knit, garden, jog; we read the comics every morning, do the crossword puzzle every night.[109]

Although Wolf is pointing out that one may engage in more than a single project that adds meaning to one's life, she is not claiming that all of these facets of life mentioned above generate meaning. She is referring to activities that fall into various dimensions of a good life—happiness, morality, and meaning.

If I am correct that worthwhileness is established by the ways in which focal things reach out into, and connect, their contexts, and if active engagement is required, then distraction from this activity can be disastrous in our attempts to create meaning. Take the case of the carpenter who is meeting with a customer to discuss a commissioned cabinet. This interaction establishes a social connection on the basis of which an aspect of the worthwhileness of the project is generated. The carpenter is passionate about her own work and her finished products, but this interaction with her customer is one place where her work becomes worthwhile outside of herself. If smartphone-distraction (a notification, say) pulls the carpenter out of the developing experience that grounds this conversation, this distraction puts at risk the creation of meaningfulness.

5.8 Taking Stock

Borgmann's focal things are the material anchors of focal practices. A musical instrument is a focal thing; musical performance is a focal practice. A CD player and Spotify are technological devices. A device does not require skill. In fact, devices disburden us; using Spotify saves a music enthusiast from having to learn to play a musical instrument. Another feature of devices is that their machinery is mostly hidden. Devices also disengage us from contexts. Devices have functional equivalents. Running shoes, dishwashers, and guitar amplifiers are examples of technological paraphernalia (which Borgmann calls technological "instruments") (5.4). Paraphernalia are distinct from devices and focal things. Paraphernalia support focal things and practices. This category shows that Borgmann has a favorable opinion of certain technological objects, but not devices.

Focal things have five characteristic features. Feature 1: Focal things have no functional equivalents (5.2.1). A guitar is not valuable merely as a means to procure music; if it were, it could be replaced by something else that also procures music. As it is, many of a guitar's properties are valuable, and many are context-dependent. In fact—this is feature 2—a focal thing connects a context (5.2.2). A guitar connects musicians, listeners, and audience members; it connects the guitarist and other musicians to the musical tradition, and perhaps to the broader community. All of Borgmann's focal practices draw upon social contexts (e.g., the culture of the table), natural contexts (e.g., hiking), or both (the practice centered on the fireplace). Feature 3: Focal things make demands on us; they require patience, attention, and skill (5.2.3). When an audience member encounters musical instruments at a musical performance this requires informed, active listening skills.

The fourth characteristic feature of focal things is that they are inconspicuous (5.2.4). Great artworks in pretechnological epochs, such as a Greek temple, could provide a paradigm for an entire culture, according to Heidegger. We have seen that focal things have the capacity to center one's life (5.5), which is a related capacity. In our contemporary culture, the things that have the capacity to orient our lives in this way are ordinary, and in some way unremarkable objects, such as meals, running-paths, fishing rods, and musical instruments. Feature 5: Although inconspicuous, focal things are unprocurable in the sense that they seem inexhaustible and continually challenging (5.2.5). This is not merely due to their own properties but due to their possibilities which arise through their context-dependence. Through skillful engagement, a good musician can bring out of her instrument unexpected expressiveness. Such possibilities are multiplied through the interactions of a musical group.

Turning to focal practices, these safeguard and preserve focal things (5.3.1). From a psychological or motivational perspective, focal practices serve as a mechanism for propping-up our engagement with focal things. I have claimed that focal practices and things are worthwhile (5.7). If this is correct, this propping-up feature is noteworthy: focal practices are not only worthwhile, they have the capacity to help us sustain engagement in creating meaningfulness.

Focal practices also protect focal things from our culture's propensity toward optimization, the tendency to convert everything into a mere resource. This is to protect focal things from what Borgmann calls, "the technological diremption into means and ends."[110] In other words, focal practices guard against one applying an efficiency-mindset to focal things such as a family dinner, which could result in one coming to prefer eating fast food or microwavable food.

Focal practices also generate value through their procedures, norms, and traditions (5.3.2). In certain cases, such as where the focal thing is the path of a run, the focal thing does not enter the practice as already valuable (as does the focal thing in hiking, which is the wilderness). Instead, the focal thing acquires its value through the practice's procedures, norms, and traditions.

Focal practices frame engagement in such a way that we come to conceive of focal things as worthy of our engagement as ends in themselves, not merely as means but as worthwhile (5.7). There is a more concrete way to put this. Focal practices can function as obstructions to instrumental thinking. If, for example, one attempts to engage in a family dinner merely as a mechanism for eating, the practice will "tell" you that you are doing it wrong. The norms, and the other people adhering to these norms, will get in your way of participating in the dinner as a mere means to an end.

In 2.3, I argued that engagement in meaningful activities cannot be understood in terms of means and ends. Although focal practices protect against instrumental thinking, they can also be endangered by it. One danger is that instrumental thinking leads us to conceive of the value of focal things and practices in terms of an end product, which, from a capitalist perspective, one may conceive of as a commodity (5.3.1).[111] Consider the following, related danger. The very studies on smartphone-distraction we considered in 2.1 and 2.2 not only embody an incorrect manner of understanding smartphone-distraction within focal practices, but are also a danger to focal practices, in one important sense. To take the education example, these studies treat instrumental thinking as if it were the proper way to understand and engage in classroom experiences (paying attention to a teacher in order to learn, which is then cashed out in terms of exams and grades).[112] But one can also engage in a philosophy seminar as a focal practice, and this meaningful engagement could be undercut by such instrumental thinking. I will discuss this example further in Chapter 6.

Sociality, which is a central part of some focal practices, seems to be valuable in itself (5.3.4). The pandemic that began in 2019 has reminded us of the meaningfulness of physically being with others. Social interaction also contributes to the value of a focal practice in other ways; for example, sociality extends one's capabilities. In musical performance, consider the metaphor of conversation among musicians and with an audience.

Focal things and practices can center one's life (5.5). We have encountered the way in which focal things can center a context. A hearth connects a home context; a guitar connects a performance context. This gathered context is the ground of centering. But what is centering more broadly? Borgmann believes that when one is dedicated to a focal practice it can inform other aspects of one's life in the sense that the practice can cast a certain interpretive order on a person's life, where what is central to the practice *colors* various other life experiences, giving them a unifying center. Borgmann says that a focal practice "is a final and dominant end which alone truly matters and fulfills and which therefore assigns all other things and activities their rank and place."[113] In a remark about music, he is even more concrete about the way in which a focal practice might center one's life: "A focal practice is one that can center and illuminate our lives. Music certainly has that power if it is alive as a regular and skillful engagement of body and mind and if it graces us in a full and final way. Our daily and mundane endeavors are then centered around music and invigorated by it."[114] And as we have seen, it may be two or three particularly compatible focal practices that center one's life.

I have employed the notion of developed experience to unpack one central aspect of effective engagement with focal things and practices. How could one effectively engage with a focal practice if one is passively drifting, with experiences being stunted due to inner lethargy or interruption? One cannot engage effectively with a focal practice by means of a passive experience nor a merely recognitional experience. I offer developed experience as a kind of experience that can contribute to meaningfulness. Dewey helps us to understand the step-by-step process of interaction, through his description of the experiential phases of doing, undergoing, and the importance of one's awareness of the relations among these phases. Through his concepts of pervasive quality and consummation, Dewey gives us a way of conceiving of aspects of an experience that are qualitatively unified and ultimately satisfying. These are some of the observations that lead me to the claim that engaging with focal things and practice by means of developed experiences can generate meaning in one's life. My connection of developed experience to Wolf's subjective condition (4.3), and my connection of focal things and practices to Wolf's objective condition (5.7), provide additional support for this claim.

In 5.7, I argue that in order to satisfy Wolf's objective condition an activity must have value that is "independent of oneself," as Wolf says. This is what it means for an activity to be worthwhile. Meaningfulness requires getting outside of oneself, establishing connections to one's milieu. We can elucidate this notion of worthwhileness through Borgmann's focal things and practices insofar as we can see focal things piecing-together their worthwhileness by reaching out into their context.

In a crossword competition, a crossword puzzle is a focal thing that not only engages our skills, but also connects a context, especially a social context, which establishes value for the participants. The engagement with some focal things, such as the wilderness (in hiking), seems worthwhile in itself. Other focal things, such as the path of a run, become worthwhile due to the procedures, standards, and traditions of a focal practice (5.3.1, 5.3.2, 5.7). We have also learned that focal practices have the capacity to center one's life; this value is not generated entirely by an individual's activity but is made possible by the focal practice (5.5).

If I am right about the connection between developed experience and effective engagement with focal things and practices, then what I have said about the ways in which certain smartphone-use may interfere with developing experiences (3.7) gives us a clear picture of the ways in which smartphone-use may interfere with one's engagement with focal things and practices—that is, the ways in which smartphone-use may interfere with generating meaning in life. Interruptions prevent experiences from developing. Any interruption—even something as subtle as a vibrating notification in one's phone—if it prevents one from adequately perceiving doings, undergoings, and the relations involved, then it can prevent an experience from developing. I should emphasize that the intrusion of notifications makes smartphone-distraction a potential concern within focal practices that may seem somewhat untouched by intimate technologies, such as running, fly-fishing, and hiking (the distractive potential of smart-watches also looms here). As I said in 3.7, after being distracted, one cannot simply return one's attention to a developing experience. One cannot pop in and out of a developing experience. The elements that make it the experience it potentially is are developing and integrated. Even in the basic examples that Dewey discusses we see that a given *doing* is related to a previous and subsequent *undergoing* in a way that each must be perceived without artificially imposed pauses. This becomes especially vivid when we recall that what makes a developed experience the experience that it is, what unifies it, is a pervasive quality that is present in all of the phases of the experience (at least in an incipient form), and culminates in giving the consummation its character (3.5, 3.6). Such qualitative development cannot survive a looking-away, a turning-back. Recall Dewey's concern about the damage that modern life can inflict upon the richness of experience: "We put our hands to the plow and turn back; we start and then we stop, not because the experience has reached the end for the sake of which it was initiated but because of extraneous interruptions or of inner lethargy."[115]

In the penultimate paragraph of 2.3, I raised a particularly practical question. Consider various focal-practice contexts such as a family dinner, a small arts performance, a hike, or a university seminar. What can we say to another person to convey the dangers of smartphone-use in these contexts? In 2.3, I said that framing smartphone-use in terms of means and ends misses a deeper point about meaningfulness. Regarding means and ends, of course one can say that off-task smartphone-use in a seminar may come at a cost to academic performance. And smartphone-use at a dinner may prevent one from understanding an issue discussed during a dinner-conversation. But this is to conceive of the experience instrumentally, to conceive of smartphone-distraction as an interference with achieving an objective. We can now see that a broader and deeper case can be made: Put your smartphone away, we can say, or you will not be able to cultivate a developed experience. If you have a passive or merely recognitional experience in relation to the dinner conversation (say), you will not find the focal practice subjectively fulfilling. You will not be gripped by the activity by means of a passive or merely recognitional experience. In addition—regarding acting in a focal-practice context that is worthwhile in Wolf's sense—a passive or merely recognitional experience is insufficient for effectively engaging with various aspects of the focal practice; through a passive or recognitional experience, one cannot tap into a focal practice's significance. These are the building blocks of meaningfulness. Smartphone-distraction can be an obstruction to creating meaning in one's life.

We can elaborate upon the above by considering a more invested and committed way in which one can engage in a focal practice; namely, the creation of one's self-identity through engagement with a focal practice. This is the topic of our next chapter. Regarding smartphone-distraction, this topic will give us the opportunity to examine how certain smartphone-use can negatively affect social contexts, which are at the core of many focal practices.

6

Identity-Work

6.1. Introduction

In this chapter, I want to consider one way in which smartphones have altered our social environments, particularly in small-group settings. Smartphones impact small groups in many ways but the theme that I will develop here is the effect of smartphone-use upon the typically unnoticed work one does to create one's self-identity. We will be considering small-group settings organized around focal practices. While we will be considering potentially meaningful engagements, in Wolf's sense, our focus will be upon the work we do in such groups to shape our self-identities.

I will argue that certain smartphone-use tears the social fabric in ways that are detrimental to identity-work, and that this is a compelling reason to be cautious about smartphone-use in small groups. I will work with the small-group example of a college philosophy seminar, but my general contention can be extended to similar group-contexts, such as small musical performances, charity events, dinner parties, diplomatic meetings, family gatherings, and so on.

It may help to remind ourselves that I am not concerned here with the ways in which smartphone-use can interfere with the successful completion of tasks, as we discussed in Chapter 2. Even though I will be exploring the example of a philosophy seminar, I will not be focused on the potential negative impact of smartphone-use on a person's academic performance; given what we have seen in previous chapters, the negative impact of off-task smartphone-use on performance is predictable. I will not be approaching these small-group situations through a means/ends orientation.

I will draw upon the foundational existentialist claim that an individual creates her self-identity. In order to explore this with specificity, I will focus on early Heidegger. To emphasize the sense in which this identity-work is social, I will invoke Heidegger's notion of "being-with" (*Mitsein*).[1] We will see that identity-work takes place in social contexts that a group of individuals create and preserve together. I will not focus upon the identity-work of those who are using smartphones; *the focus here will be the negative impact of some individuals' smartphone-use upon the social context and the identity-work of others.*

6.2 Seminar

I want to use an example that will familiarize us with the relevant phenomena. I will return to the example throughout the chapter for illustrative purposes and also in the hope that considering these issues through a concrete example will serve as some persuasion to supplement my other reasoning. Now, imagine a college philosophy seminar consisting of approximately seventeen students sitting at a large table. Although the professor raises questions, clarifies arguments, makes interpretive claims, and occasionally reads key passages from texts, the seminar primarily operates through active discussion. Suppose that a topic has emerged that has grabbed most everyone's interest. A discussion unfolds in which students and the professor are taking turns offering points of clarification and articulating pieces of reasoning. A significant number of the students are engaged in this process, making the mood in the room lively. The professor is holding back some concluding points in order to allow the discussion to develop organically. Progress is being made. There is a sense that the group is working through a set of issues together. The students are even taking the discussion in effective directions that the professor did not anticipate, which adds a layer of gratification to the discussion, both for the professor and the students.

This particular seminar meeting, and others like it, are potentially parts of a larger focal practice. Perhaps this seminar is a part of a larger focal practice we can call philosophical discussion, where the focal things are philosophical texts (or perhaps, more abstractly, philosophical ideas or arguments). Some individuals are passionate about philosophical discussion; that is, for some, engagement in philosophical discussion is subjectively fulfilling in Wolf's sense. As a reminder, recall that passive or merely recognitional experiences are insufficient for such engagement (4.3). Also, the value of these texts, arguments, and convivial get-togethers is independent of a given individual who finds them to be subjectively fulfilling (5.7). I am suggesting that this activity (philosophy seminars, and other aspects of this focal practice) can be understood as worthwhile, meaningful for some people.[2]

Let's turn to the examination of smartphone-distraction as it relates to identity-work in this sort of small group. Imagine that one student, Emma, is attempting to articulate a complex point. She is challenging a statement in the text by drawing upon an observation made in another text. While she works through her thoughts aloud, another student—call him Joe—reaches for his smartphone, and begins off-task texting with a friend, in effect disengaging from what Emma is saying, and from the seminar in general. Like a yawn, the contagion results in two other students beginning to look at their phones.[3] Emma notices, and the behavior strikes her as impolite. Such a turn of events has become increasingly common in small groups. How can we understand what is at stake here?

6.3 Self-Identity

I want to explore the prospect that Emma is shaping an important aspect of who she is trying to become through the seminar. She is cultivating an intellectual layer of her self-identity. Emma has chosen to study philosophy, so she is developing her self as a person who employs the methodology and draws upon the history of philosophy to think about the world and her place in it. She takes studying philosophy seriously. To give it a name, let's say that Emma is a budding philosopher.[4] We can call this aspect of the work in which she is engaged identity-work. Perhaps Emma consciously looks upon philosophical discussions as potentially meaningful experiences; she is gripped by such engagements, in Wolf's sense.

A common existentialist claim is that humans do not have a general essence; we do not have a human nature. Rather, I create or shape my individual essence, my self-identity.[5] Using the term "*Dasein*" to refer to the self (roughly), Heidegger is getting at something like this when he writes, "The essence of *Dasein* lies in its existence."[6] Hubert Dreyfus emphasizes that this meaning of existence, this shaping of one's self-identity, is active and social: "To exist is to take a stand on what is essential about one's being and to be defined by that stand. Thus Dasein is what, in its social activity, it interprets itself to be."[7] For example, an individual creates her self-identity as a drummer by watching and listening to other drummers, by discussing music with other musicians, by playing music with other musicians, by playing for audiences while being affected by their reactions to the music, and so on. This person is engaging in the general focal practice of music as well as the nested focal practice of musical performance.

An individual's self-identity is not singular. An individual is not only a drummer, a budding philosopher, a runner, or a sacrificial parent; an individual's identity consists of a cluster of such roles. For example, one person might be a budding philosopher, a conscientious friend, a committed romantic partner, and an anti-gun activist. (Note that this has some resonance with Borgmann's allowance that one might center one's life through more than one focal practice. Recall that Wolf also acknowledges this plurality in the meaningful dimension of an individual's life.)

But more specifically, what I am cashing out as a role is what Heidegger refers to as a "for-the-sake-of-which."[8] The basic sense of this term is that, for instance, after her friend underwent a traumatic event, Emma calls her friend *for the sake of* being a conscientious friend. A for-the-sake-of-which is roughly a self-interpretation: Dreyfus explains, "A for-the-sake-of-which, like being a father or being a professor, is not to be thought of as a goal

I have in mind and can achieve. Indeed, it is not a goal at all, but rather a self-interpretation that informs and orders all my activities."[9]

Now, although identity-work is often deliberate, it can be less deliberate, less conscious, than one might expect. Dreyfus has raised interesting examples of identity-work that are not deliberate, such as being a sacrificial parent. Even though no one sets out to become a sacrificial parent (I presume), this self-identity is nevertheless created through various actions. Dreyfus writes:

> [F]or-the-sake-of-whichs need not be intentional at all. I pick up my most basic life-organizing self-interpretations by socialization, not by choosing them. For example, one behaves as an older brother or a mama's girl without having chosen these organizing self-interpretations, and without having them in mind as specific purposes. These ways of being lead one to certain organized activities such as being a teacher, nurse, victim, etc.[10]

Certainly, then, some identity-work can take place non-deliberately, while a person is engaging with one focal practice or another. One way to interpret Emma is simply as engaging in philosophical discussion because she is gripped by it (satisfying Wolf's subjective condition), not as deliberately trying to shape her identity. By whichever path, Emma has found herself engaging seriously in philosophy seminars, and she has a sense that this is important to her. She may consciously consider herself to be a budding philosopher or she may not. Either way, this role makes sense of the way she behaves. For example, Emma takes the textual support of the claims discussed in the seminar more seriously than some other students, even other good students. In his book, *The*

Examined Life, Robert Nozick gives us a glimpse of himself as a young person, which characterizes what it is for a philosophical text to be a focal thing for a young, budding philosopher:

> When I was fifteen years old or sixteen I carried around in the streets of Brooklyn a paperback copy of Plato's *Republic*, front cover facing outward. I had read only some of it and understood less, but I was excited by it and knew it was something wonderful.[11]

One apt aspect of this quotation is that it speaks to the unprocurability of focal things (5.2.5), and the attractiveness of this characteristic. There is an interesting sense in which a text like the *Republic* is like a musical instrument; even after many readings, it can surprise one.

The potential un-deliberateness of identity-work can be seen by noting that Emma's role may be identified by someone else before she explicitly realizes it herself. Another student might say to her—under his breath and sarcastically—"Okay, Professor." In such a moment, Emma may realize for the first time perhaps—"Oh, I do care about this more than some other students; maybe this is who I am interested in becoming."[12] Whatever the case may be, while she is doing her identity-work, she will be reflecting upon philosophical arguments but she will not be reflecting upon her budding role. She will be in a groove, absorbedly coping, as Dreyfus would say.[13]

You might think of this chapter as attempting to answer three questions; I have already suggested an answer to the first. (a) What is the import of the seminar for Emma? One valuable aspect of the seminar for Emma is that it is where and when she does certain identity-work.[14] Notice that we could just as easily be considering the identity-work accomplished in other small-group focal practices, such as musical performance or political diplomacy. The strategy of the remainder of the chapter is to answer two additional questions. (b) In what ways does Emma's identity-work depend upon others? (c) What effect does the smartphone-use of others in the seminar have upon Emma's identity-work?

6.4 Being-With

In this section, I want to answer the second question: In what ways does Emma's identity-work depend upon others? I've said that according to existential phenomenology Emma shapes her self-identity by taking certain actions in social contexts. To get a better sense of this social emphasis, I find it helpful to consider the phenomenon of *being-with* (*Mitsein*), drawing from Heidegger's *Being and Time*.

As a preliminary to being-with, consider Heidegger's notion of *world*. The world is not a thing, not a place, but rather a context in which I am involved. To get a sense of what a Heideggerian world is, consider the academic world of our example. We can think of the academic world as a microcosm of Heidegger's broader notion of world.[15] The academic world is made up of individuals occupying various roles (or we might say, enacting various self-interpretations), such as attentive students, budding philosophers, class clowns, teachers, program assistants, and deans. These roles are related in various ways, and they are grounded on practices generally. Further, students and teachers use items such as pens, books, notebooks, seminar-room tables, chairs, chalkboards, and attendance sheets. This equipment *(Zeug)*, to use Heidegger's term, and the ways in which these items are related, are part of what constitutes the academic world.

Heidegger believes that we can render intelligible and grasp the significance of equipment, human roles, and practices, by clarifying relations, by articulating the structure of the world, which he calls *worldhood*. Dreyfus walks us through an example: "I write on the blackboard in a classroom, with a piece of chalk, in order to draw a chart, as a step towards explaining Heidegger, for the sake of my being a good teacher."[16] He continues: "The intelligibility of a piece of chalk is that it is used in order to write on blackboards; the point of writing on the board with a piece of chalk is tied in to practices necessary for a self-interpretation, such as being a teacher."[17] I want to extract a straightforward point from the above: In cultivating the role of a budding philosopher, Emma relies upon this context of equipment as well as the social aspect of the context. These roles, and this equipment, have the significance they do because of this social context, this academic world.

Heidegger famously claims that you and I (*Dasein*) are *being-in-the-world*. He does not intend the "in" in a spatial sense, like being in a room. Rather, the "in" refers to the fact that I am necessarily involved in the world. Similarly, when Heidegger claims that Dasein is being-with, the "with" does not mean that other individuals are here with me, in the sense of being physically present.[18] Rather, "being-with" refers to our underlying involvement with others.[19] As William Blattner provisionally defines it, "'being-with' is Heidegger's term for the background way in which we share the world with others."[20] (Relatedly, Heidegger refers to the being of others as *Dasein-with* [*Mitdasein*], which is intended to highlight the fact that this underlying involvement is not a being-with things or equipment but with other *Dasein*.)[21]

In other words, I am being-with, which is ontological, even in a particular situation in which I am physically alone—this latter, particular and concrete level of description is what Heidegger refers to as "ontic."[22] Heidegger writes, "Even *Dasein*'s Being-alone is Being-with in the world. The Other can be missing only *in* and *for* a Being-with. Being-alone is a deficient mode of Being-with."[23] Heidegger fleshes-out the character of being-with through the observation that our underlying ontological orientation or relation toward others is one of solicitude (*Fürsorge*). The ontological/ontic distinction is important regarding solicitude because Heidegger does not mean that we always care for particular others (again, this particularity is ontic). In fact, Heidegger believes that we are typically not solicitous of others; instead, we tend to be indifferent to others, disrespectful, inconsiderate, and so on:

> *Dasein* maintains itself proximally and for the most part in the deficient modes of solicitude. Being for, against, or without one another, passing one another by, not "mattering" to one another—these are possible ways of solicitude. And it is precisely these last-named deficient and indifferent modes that characterize everyday, average Being-with-one-another.[24]

Now, the Heideggerian world is a social context that we utilize and rely upon together. Consider the shared nature of the assigned text on this day in the seminar. Let's say the text is Borgmann's *Technology and the Character of Contemporary Life*. Emma is focused on the book in asking a question (she might read aloud a short passage of the text to support an interpretive point she has made); the teacher is also focused on the text in answering the question (the teacher may read another passage). The students and teacher also share the equipment of the university, the classroom, and they lean on the same seminar-room table. In addition, each student is shaping her own role in the same public context that is made up of the same equipment, the same general roles, and the same practices.

But it is not only the case that we use and rely upon the same social context; Emma's identity-work and the identity-work of others is intertwined; their identity-work is, in fact, interdependent. The work she is engaged in to shape her identity is interwoven with the identity-work of others. For example, my identity-work in sustaining or developing my identity as a philosophy teacher is interwoven with Emma's identity-work in establishing her identity as a budding philosopher. And the identity-work of one budding philosopher, Emma, is intertwined with the identity-work of another budding philosopher in the seminar, Khiry, and another merely strategic learner, Frank. Consider Blattner's and then Dreyfus's comments about the necessarily social dimension of identity-work:

> In confronting the question of my identity, I am also confronting the question of the identity of others. . . . I cannot disentangle who I am from who those around me are. . . . As I go about being a father, teacher, and neighbor, how those with whom I engage in being all these things understand themselves is not irrelevant to me. That my sons respond to my fathering by being adoring children, that some of my students respond to my teaching by dedicating themselves to their studies, is crucially important to me in so far as I am a father and teacher.[25]

> Dasein is always interpreting its being in term[s] of its for-the-sake-of-whichs, and since one's role, say that of being a professor, makes no sense without other roles, like that of being a student,

as well as meshing with still other roles such as being a teaching assistant, librarian, advisor, registrar, etc., we cannot even make sense of a nonsocial Dasein.[26]

Recall our second question—In what ways does Emma's identity work depend upon others? We find an answer in the interdependency of identity-work. In the seminar, Emma cannot effectively shape her role as a budding philosopher—she cannot effectively conduct her identity-work—without some others in the seminar conducting their own identity-work. Perhaps it does not matter which others are conducting their own identity-work, because, setting aside what might be interesting and helpful to her, what is necessary is that the group-context be preserved. Among other contexts, Emma relies upon a functioning seminar context for her identity-work.[27]

What is crucial for the kinds of identity-work I am considering is not merely the ontological structure of being-with but the ontic, particular concrete ways in which individuals relate to one another, their "modes of solicitude." The seminar context cannot be sustained through entirely deficient modes of solicitude. Emma relies upon a seminar context in which she is understood, engaged with, and intellectually challenged by the other students as well as the teacher.

We should continue to emphasize the context. Consider some of the contextual requirements of this small group. If there are not a sufficient number of students in the seminar who have completed the reading in advance of the session, then a serious discussion cannot take root. Further, some students must be following the finer points of the teacher's explication of the arguments in order for the students to be able to understand and engage with Emma's complex comments. It is not the case that Emma's identity-work requires every other student in the seminar to be cultivating the identity of a budding philosopher. But if most of the other students are working toward identities like "class clown" or "cool and detached," then the kind of intellectual interaction Emma relies upon to pursue her identity-work in the seminar will not be available, and at some level of general detachment this will simply cease to be a functioning seminar context. And of course we should not let the teacher off the hook. Such students' identity-work also depends upon the teacher doing her own complementary identity-work. If the teacher does not take the students seriously enough— if she does not sufficiently challenge them—then it will not be possible for Emma to conduct effective identity-work by means of the seminar. Ultimately, to effectively accomplish her identity-work in the seminar, Emma relies upon the functioning of the context, which is concretely constituted by, and sustained by, these others occupying the requisite roles.

Above, I answered our second question in a second-person manner, by focusing upon the interdependency of Emma's and others' roles in the seminar. For our purposes of considering the effects of smartphones in small groups, it is, indeed, helpful to highlight the relationships between smartphone-users and others engaged in identity-work. But ultimately, what Emma relies upon is not so much specific individuals but having access to a functioning social context (which is created and maintained by some others). The most straightforward way, therefore, to answer our second question is to focus on the negative effects of smartphone-use by some upon the social context. Take our second question again. In what ways does Emma's identity work depend upon others? In order to conduct her identity-work in the seminar, the seminar context must be effectively functioning; others create and sustain this context along with Emma.

Whether we consider philosophy seminars, small musical performances, or a series of meetings among diplomats, there will be a threshold of engagement—in the activity that makes the group the group that it is—which must be met by members of the group in order to create and preserve the group's social context. And in order for a member of a group to engage in effective identity-work, the group's social context must be preserved. There are many ways in which members of a small group might disengage from the group's social context. Next, we will consider one, increasingly ubiquitous way in which individuals disengage from groups, smartphone-use.

6.5 Smartphones and Group Context

Recall our third question: What effect does the smartphone-use of others in the seminar have upon Emma's identity-work? Consider this answer: If smartphone-use results in disengagement from the group's defining activity (the activity that makes the group the group that it is), and if this disengagement leads to a failure to preserve the group's context, then the interactions Emma relies upon to pursue her identity-work in the seminar will not be available. One way students in a seminar can be disengaged is by texting, engaging with social media, and so on. To generalize, off-task smartphone-use by some individuals in small-groups can be detrimental to the identity-work of others.[28]

Is this correct? Consider an objection from the perspective of one student in the seminar, Joe. Joe might claim that he is able to use his smartphone, and at the same time, remain sufficiently engaged in the seminar. He believes he can read and write texts on his smartphone while keeping enough of his attention on the work of the seminar in order to play his part in preserving the seminar context.

In Chapter 2, we worked through the issues that enable us to reply to Joe's objection. We can begin by recapitulating some observations about perceptual structure. When Joe is sitting across from Emma, focusing on her articulation of her argument, Emma, and her claims and reasoning, are in the foreground of his experience. In the background are the trees through the window, other students, the sounds in the hall, and so on. When Joe begins texting, Emma and her ideas recede into the background; the person with whom Joe is texting, and that person's ideas and questions, surge into the foreground. Joe becomes more engaged with his texting-friend than he is with Emma, even if his friend is six-thousand miles away.[29] Joe disengages from his immediate context while texting, insofar as his immediate context recedes into the background. If Joe experiences Emma's articulation of her argument as a background experience only, he will likely not be able to engage with it.[30]

Granting that he cannot effectively attend to Emma *while* he is texting, Joe might reply to the points above by claiming that he can control his attention, shifting back and forth rapidly at-will. This shifting enables him, he says, to give sufficient attention both to his texting and the seminar discussion. We can draw upon our examination of multitasking in Chapter 2 in order to address Joe's claims. The core of our reply is that what Joe suggests he can do is strong multitasking (2.4), which is made even more difficult in light of the phenomena of sedimentation and dominant stability

(2.5). The strong multitasking would come at too great a cost to engagement in the seminar. To invoke Diane Michelfelder's example from Chapter 2, participating in a text conversation with a friend while engaging in a philosophy seminar is more like using one hand to steer a vacuum cleaner across the floor while using the other to brush one's teeth than it is like holding a conversation with a passenger while driving on a country road. The latter is weak multitasking. Texting while engaging in a philosophy seminar are contradictory activities, requiring strong multitasking. Joe's suggestion that he can rapidly shift his attention is not viable.

I began this section by answering our third question in this way: If smartphone-use leads to a degree of disengagement from the group's defining activity such that the group-context cannot be preserved, then the interactions Emma relies upon for pursuing her identity-work in the seminar will not be available. Just above, I have focused on considering one individual using a smartphone, and I have given reasons to believe that when an individual participates in a text conversation he would disengage from the seminar context to the extent that he would fail to support that context and thereby fail to support Emma's identity-work.

As I have said above, for the purposes of this chapter, our focus can shift away from one individual toward the group context. A philosophy seminar is a certain kind of context in which we do certain kinds of work. As long as the context is functioning and available for Emma to engage with, individual contributions to the context can vary. We can obviously have a functioning philosophy-seminar context in which many students are not budding philosophers (some students can be strategic learners and others can be struggling with the material). But pervasive disengagement can result in the context breaking down. And we are here considering the way in which this disengagement can be brought on by certain smartphone-use (the afore-mentioned contagion of smartphone-use is relevant here).

Exactly what is required for the seminar context to be preserved? This cannot be determined abstractly; the answer will depend upon the particular group, the material being discussed, and so on. In addition, different individuals will have different needs for effectively accomplishing identity-work. The context Emma needs will depend upon how many philosophy courses she has taken, how sensitive she is to being ignored, her mood on a given day, and so on.[31] What we can say abstractly is that the kind of identity-work we are considering depends upon a social context, it depends upon others, and when more than a small percentage of the group disengages from this kind of context, it is likely to have a negative effect on identity-work.

With this focus on group contexts, we can ask whether individual smartphone-users have a responsibility of some sort to particular other individuals in a group when the latter are attempting to do identity-work. Maybe they do, but it seems more straightforward to claim that individuals have a responsibility to the group. Upon joining such a group, perhaps each person should be understood to be accepting some responsibility to play her part in preserving the group context. This context is important for individuals at least insofar as it is by means of this context that a person can engage in identity-work. When a person makes the decision to join a seminar or a performance he is making a commitment to others in the group to do his part to sustain the social context.[32]

Recall the examples of other kinds of small groups I have mentioned: a small musical performance, a small charity event, a dinner party, a family gathering in the home, a meeting of diplomats, and so on. In each of these cases, will smartphone users likely disengage from the group's social context, and so potentially have a negative effect on the identity-work of others? One way to determine the precise sense in which these groups are analogous to the seminar is to consider whether (a) texting or other off-task smartphone-use and (b) engaging with the group will require managing conflicting activities, that is, whether this requires strong multitasking (2.4). If so, then the concerns articulated above are echoed.

6.6 Taking Stock

A particular small-group meeting such as a philosophy seminar, a diplomatic meeting, a charity event, or a small musical performance may be key components of a focal practice (5.3, 6.2). That is, in addition to the ordinary ways in which we classify a philosophy seminar, it may be considered a part of a focal practice that we can call philosophical discussion. Such meetings may be subjectively fulfilling for the individuals involved, in Wolf's sense. I have argued that this requires experiences that are active beyond mere recognitional experiential activity, and I have suggested that the notion of developed experience provides a useful model (Chapter 2, 4.3). Like other focal practices, one can make the case that these focal practices are worthwhile independently of a given individual's positive subjective attitude toward them (5.7). These are potentially meaningful activities.

There is an important point that I have left unsaid in this chapter: If you find yourself in such a context, and you are engaging in strong multitasking with off-task smartphone-use, this is bound to negatively affect *your own* identity-work. Rather than this personal situation, I have focused on the more complex case of the negative impact of some individuals' smartphone-use upon the social context and the identity-work of others. We worked with the case of a student in a philosophy seminar, Emma, a budding philosopher, whose identity-work is negatively affected in the seminar by Joe and some other students who use their phones for off-task purposes, such as having text conversations (6.2–6.3). This chapter turns on the existentialist view that one shapes one's self-identity in social contexts. We each cultivate multiple roles (a role is roughly what Dreyfus takes to be a self-interpretation; Heidegger calls this, roughly, a "for-the-sake-of-which"). Identity-work may or may not be deliberate.

In 6.3, I ask the question—What is the import of the seminar for Emma? One significant aspect of the seminar for her is that it is one place where she does identity-work. Anyone might engage in a handful of focal practices, but some practices will be more consequential than others. For example, Emma may have a friend who takes her hiking a few times each year, but hiking is not nearly as important to Emma as the focal practice we are calling philosophical discussion. Perhaps Emma hikes primarily to spend time with her hiking-enthusiast friend. I am suggesting that the focal practices that really matter to one may be the practices in which one does identity-work.[33] Perhaps we can put this in Borgmann's terms by saying that these select practices are the ones that center one's life (5.5 and 5.6). Borgmann also maintains that that engagement with focal things and practices "molds the person and gives the person character."[34] Shaping one's identity through a focal practice adds a certain profundity to the meaning one creates through the engagement with focal things and practices. One stakes one's claim, so to speak, on this meaning-generating context. In "The Meanings of Lives," Wolf relates self-identity to meaningfulness. The topic of self-identity emerges in Wolf's analysis of an alienated housewife:

> [S]he buys groceries and fixes meals, cleans the house, does the laundry, chauffeurs the children from school to soccer to ballet, arranges doctors' appointments and babysitters. What makes her life insufficiently meaningful is that her heart, so to speak, isn't in these activities.[35]

What does it mean for her heart not to be in it? "She does not identify with what she is doing—she does not embrace her roles as wife, mother, and home-maker as expressive of who she is and wants to be."[36] (Note the use of "role.") In a footnote to this passage, Wolf sounds even more like Heidegger and Dreyfus; she remarks that meaningful projects are those that "contribute to the unity of the life or of a significant stage of it," which she unpacks as a project "being a basis for 'making sense' of the life."[37] This calls to mind Heidegger's "for-the-sake-of-which," which Dreyfus characterizes as a self-interpretation.

In 6.4, I ask the question—In what ways does Emma's identity-work depend upon others? To effectively pursue the role of budding philosopher, Emma needs the interaction of some other students and a teacher. Similarly, a person pursuing the role of a parent needs interaction with a child. Much of the identity-work one does is intertwined with the identity-work of others. As Blattner puts it, "I cannot disentangle who I am from who those around me are."[38] In 6.4 I find detailed support for this maneuver by working with Heidegger's notion of being-with. The interdependence of identity-work frames the answer to the question about the sense in which Emma's identity-work is dependent upon others. Emma cannot effectively shape her role as a budding philosopher without some others in the seminar conducting their own identity-work.

Toward the end of 6.4, I shift the emphasis away from Emma's reliance on particular others, and toward her reliance on a functioning seminar context. Emma needs the seminar to be an effectively functioning seminar, and it will not be if most of the other students are disengaged. One way to be disengaged from the seminar is to be distracted by off-task use of one's smartphone. The issue then becomes whether individuals, like Joe, contribute to the breakdown of the seminar context or preserve it. Emma's identity-work depends upon this context. Off-task smartphone-use by some individuals in small-groups can be detrimental to the identity-work of others. Does Joe have a responsibility to support Emma's identity-work? I prefer the position that Joe, having joined the seminar, has a responsibility to contribute to its preservation (6.5). In fact, aside from our focus here upon identity-work, we might make the same claim about an individual's responsibility to preserve a focal practice that he has joined.

In 6.5, we revisit some of the arguments in Chapter 2, but this time, they are concretely considered in light of our example. I argue that Joe cannot have an off-task text conversation while remaining effectively engaged in the seminar. I argue that participating in a text conversation while engaging with a seminar is strong multitasking (2.4), which is not viable, and would result in a significant cost to effective engagement in the seminar. Joe's attempting to text and engage in the seminar would be made more difficult due to the phenomena of sedimentation and dominant stability (2.5).

Returning to the health of the social context, what is required for the preservation of the context cannot be determined abstractly.

We cannot say, for instance, that if a certain percentage of students begin texting, then the context will fail to function effectively. There are too many context-dependent factors at play, such as the dynamics of a particular group, the material being discussed, and so on. The degree of support Emma needs to effectively accomplish her identity-work also depends upon concrete and contextual details (6.5).

I close by suggesting that there is a straightforward way to apply this same reasoning to other group contexts, such as a small musical performance, a small charity event, a dinner party, a family gathering in the home, a meeting of diplomats, and so on. Smartphone-use will negatively affect a group context, and so identity-work in a given group, when engagement in the group and the smartphone-activity under consideration require strong multitasking. The question turns on whether the two activities are contradictory or complementary (2.4). Note that the focal practice of musical performance, which we discussed in Chapter 5, if it is small, is similar in many ways to a seminar. Identity-work is being accomplished by music enthusiasts as well as musicians, and a functioning context is required for these individuals to do this work. In a small performance, off-task smartphone use can have a negative effect on the context—the same can be said for a small dance performance, a small improv show, and so on. To return to what was left unsaid in this chapter, we did not consider the meaning-creation or identity-work of Joe, the person using his phone for off-task texting. If Joe is failing to support the focal-practice context due to a lack of engagement, his own experiences are interrupted; his own cultivation of meaning, his own identity-work, will not get off the ground.

7

A Note of Cautious Optimism

In this book, my aim has been to reveal the often-hidden impact of smartphone-distraction upon meaningful experiences, activities, projects, and identity-work. We should be more sensitive to, and supportive of, focal-practice contexts. In the short term, I believe we should put our smartphones away when we encounter a potential source of meaning, whether the source is a small social context, an encounter with another person, or with nature. Merely putting our smartphones away, however, may not be enough because notifications, which solicit off-task smartphone-use, persist. In light of this concern, cultivating a proactive habit of employing a "do not disturb" feature is helpful.

Perhaps we can begin the difficult work of identifying, loosening, and reshaping our sedimented smartphone habits, which currently pull us away from the kind of engagement needed for fostering developed experiences (2.5, Chapter 3). This work might be aided by changes in smartphone design and app design. In this regard, it may be helpful briefly to unspool a few ideas from previous chapters. Recall Borgmann's concept of *technological paraphernalia*, which I raised in 5.4.[1] Reminding ourselves of the following

Borgmannian categories will help: A turntable (or a full stereo set) is a technological device (5.2.1); a guitar is a focal thing (5.2); I contend that a guitar amplifier and a microphone are technological paraphernalia. Technological paraphernalia are pieces of technology, which, unlike devices, *support* focal things and practices. As Borgmann says, technological paraphernalia "call forth" engagement with a focal thing and in a focal practice.[2] Borgmann's example of technological paraphernalia are running shoes, which support the focal practice of running. Dreyfus and Spinosa also explore the usefulness of technological paraphernalia, mentioning the example of a dishwasher, which can support the focal practice of a family dinner (5.4).

One way to consider what would be involved in effectively incorporating smartphones into meaningful activities is to ask this question: In university seminars, small musical performances, family dinners, and other focal-practice contexts, *what would it take for a smartphone to function effectively as technological paraphernalia?* Since a smartphone can be used in so many ways, the answer depends upon how the smartphone is used. We can eliminate off-task smartphone-use straightaway. Off-task smartphone-use does not call forth or support engagement with a focal practice. In fact, off-task smartphone-use pulls one away from a focal-practice context (see 2.1, 2.2, 6.6). Choosing to use a smartphone for off-task purposes in these contexts is not only to forego potential meaningfulness, it is potentially to interfere with the meaning-creation of others (we saw a particularly stark example of this in Chapter 6, in terms of identity-work). Drawing the off-task/on-task distinction, we must focus on the latter. But recall that the distractive potential of smartphones is a concern even regarding on-task use (2.4–2.6). One concern here comes from what we learned in 2.2: Since smartphones afford so many tempting use-options, it is possible that a user may be drawn rapidly and unwittingly from on-task use to off-task use. Changes in app and phone design may help to reduce the likelihood of such problems. Again, effectively employing a "do not disturb" feature is one way to prevent at least external solicitations to off-task activity.

In order for smartphones to effectively function as paraphernalia, social norms would have to shift. One example of what I mean is that even if a smartphone-user intends to support a focal-practice context, it is possible that individuals in situations like Emma's (6.5) will be thrown off their own identity-work by feeling ignored, de-valued, or disrespected when a person in her focal-practice context turns to his phone. Engaging in a particularly social focal practice requires demonstrating to the others involved that one does not have "one foot out the door"; one must demonstrate a degree of commitment. This is a part of what it means to support the context. An individual in Emma's situation would need to have many experiences in which a person looking at his phone is engaged and doing on-task work, and is attending to what she says, before she is in a position not to be thrown off by the smartphone-use of others.[3]

Setting these concerns aside, again, what exactly would it mean for a smartphone to function as paraphernalia that supports engagement in a focal practice? Recall that we are not considering support merely in the sense of helping one to achieve a goal (2.3); we are wondering whether smartphones can support *engagement* with an integrated context. We must avoid conceiving of a smartphone as a mere tool. I mean to echo Don Ihde's influential observation that even seemingly simple tools *mediate* our relationship to the world, and in different ways.[4] That is, technological paraphernalia alter the ways in which we experience and engage with our contexts. Imagining a runner's period of adjustment to new running shoes gives us a sense of the ways in which running shoes impact the runner's experience and movements; the shoes literally come between the runner and the focal thing, the path of the run. We have to be cautious that when we believe smartphone-use is supporting an aspect of engagement in a context, it does not close us off from, or negatively reshape, other aspects of the focal-practice context in a way that interferes with the cultivation of meaningfulness.

Additionally, how can smartphone-use be integrated into one's active, developing experiences within a focal-practice context? What would it look like for the doings, undergoings, and the awareness of relations of a developing experience to involve smartphone-use seamlessly and in a way that a fragile, pervasive quality is sustained? If the reader is uncomfortable with the notion of a pervasive quality, the point can be put in other terms: We should consider whether the specific character of an extended experience in a focal-practice context might be altered in a negative way by smartphone-use.

Recall that one feature of Borgmann's *devices* is that they do not demand skill, patience, and attention—focal things do. This lack of demands, which we find in devices, breeds disengagement. Perhaps some paraphernalia do make demands on us, and perhaps such demands would foster engagement in the focal practice at issue. A guitarist, for instance, must learn how to get the sounds she wants from a particular amplifier; this project is context-sensitive and challenging. Regarding microphones, a singer learns the differences between a Shure SM58 and an SM57, in terms of where to place one's lips while singing certain consonants or singing at one volume or another. It is possible that the demands that such paraphernalia make upon us draw us *into* the focal practice, insofar as the on-task work with the paraphernalia engages us. Regarding paraphernalia generally, this is promising.

Ultimately, we need to examine smartphones as objects as well as to examine particular apps. Late in his 1984 book, Borgmann implies that writing philosophy is a focal practice.[5] Can a case be made that the relevant focal things in this practice are not exactly things but descriptions, concepts, and arguments? Perhaps, more generally, the focal thing is the text. Whatever the case may be, perhaps certain smartphone writing apps can be classified as paraphernalia that call forth engagement in focal practices of writing.

Consider the app, Scrivener, which can be used on a smartphone or tablet (although it is primarily designed for computers).[6] Scrivener is complex; it has many, integrated and deep features that make demands on a writer. Does such an app make demands on the writer that call forth engagement in the writing project? Here is a reason to believe it does. By revealing and emphasizing the *structure* of a writing project, Scrivener draws one into the project. The writer is encouraged to interact with the project's structure more so than in traditional word-processing apps. The book you are reading, for example, in Scrivener, has dozens of separate sections which exist as individual files; the files show up as items in a hierarchical sidebar list that can be organized and reorganized (on the computer version, these individual items can also be viewed as virtual "notecards" with synopses). As I write, I face this structure repeatedly; this gives me a holistic and involved perspective on the project. This seems promising in understanding

Scrivener on my phone to be technological paraphernalia that calls forth my engagement in the writing project.[7] There are, of course, obvious downsides to writing on one's phone, such as the small screen size (which results in my using Scrivener primarily on my computer). Further, although it is difficult for most of us to imagine these days, writing with a pen and paper had its benefits as well; it gave us a bodily, tactile connection to the writing that we have all but lost. Ultimately, we need to assess such trade-offs in terms of the cultivation of meaningfulness.

But what are we *giving up* when we attempt to use our smartphones less often and more judiciously? Aren't many of our interactions with our smartphones indeliberate reflexes? We often turn to our phones in order to stave off boredom and social discomfort. Perhaps there is a modicum of pleasure to be gained from such smartphone experiences as scrolling through social media while waiting for an elevator. Pleasure is not nothing—recall Susan Wolf's claim that a good life has three dimensions: happiness (characterized in terms of hedonism), morality, and meaningfulness. What we have been concerned with in this book is how and in what circumstances smartphones interfere with the cultivation of meaning in our lives. My hope is that what we have worked through in these pages situates smartphones in a thought-provoking frame, helping us to think about integrating smartphones into our lives with thoughtful consideration for our selves, others, and the preservation of meaningful contexts.

Notes

1 Introduction

1   Where appropriate, I will use "activities" as shorthand for *activities, experiences, and projects.*

2   Regarding sporting events, cf. Albert Borgmann, *Crossing the Postmodern Divide* (Chicago: University of Chicago Press, 1992), 143. I am reminded of the way in which baseball functions as meaningful for the Braverman family in the television series *Parenthood*, which is brought home explicitly in the final episode of the series. Regarding musical performance, see Chapter 5.

3   John Dewey, *Art as Experience* (New York: Perigee, 1980), 36.

4   Cf. John Dewey, *Art as Experience*, 36, 37, 42 ff.

2 Distraction

1   The man, who had dementia, came to the hospital to have his feeding tube replaced (the percutaneous endoscopic gastrostomy tube, aka PEG).

2   John Halamka, "Order Interrupted by Text: Multitasking Mishap," *Patient Safety Network*, 2011. December 1, 2011.

3   Halamka, "Order Interrupted by Text: Multitasking Mishap."

4   "[T]he patient developed shortness of breath, tachycardia, and hypotension (low blood pressure). An echocardiogram revealed hemopericardium (blood filling the sack around the heart) with evidence of tamponade (pressure from the blood limiting his heart function). He required emergency open

heart surgery (pericardiocentesis and pericardial window) to remove the blood. His INR was 8.5 at the time, indicating he was overanticoagulated—his blood was too thin. The team felt he had suffered spontaneous bleeding into the pericardium from receiving the extra doses of warfarin." Halamka, "Order Interrupted by Text: Multitasking Mishap."

5   Matt Richtel, "As Doctors Use More Devices, Potential for Distraction Grows," *New York Times,* December 14, 2011.

6   Matt Richtel, "Multitasking Doctor Imperils Patient, Case Study Says." *New York Times,* January 3, 2012.

7   "Most nurses (78.1%) uses [sic] the internet for personal purposes during working hours (McBride et al., 2015a), regardless of age and professional status, with negative consequences on interdisciplinary communication and nurses' performance (Fujino & Kawamoto, 2013)." Massimo Fiorinelli et al., "Smartphone Distraction During Nursing Care: Systematic Literature Review," *Applied Nursing Research* 58 (2021): 4.

8   Gianluca Pucciarelli et al., "Nursing-Related Smartphone Activities in the Italian Nursing Population," *CIN: Computers, Informatics, Nursing* 37, no. 1 (2019): 29.

9   Sumi Cho and Eunjoo Lee, "Distraction By Smartphone Use During Clinical Practice and Opinions About Smartphone Restriction Policies: A Cross-Sectional Descriptive Study of Nursing Students," *Nurse Education Today* 40 (2016): 132.

10 T. Smith, E. Darling, and B. Searles, "2010 Survey on Cell Phone Use While Performing Cardiopulmonary Bypass," *Perfusion* 26, no. 5 (2011): 375.

11 Cho and Lee, "Distraction By Smartphone Use During Clinical Practice and Opinions About Smartphone Restriction Policies: A Cross-Sectional Descriptive Study of Nursing Students," 132.

12 This becomes directly relevant for us in Chapter 6 while considering the identity-work of Emma.

13 Cho and Lee, "Distraction By Smartphone Use During Clinical Practice and Opinions About Smartphone Restriction Policies: A Cross-Sectional Descriptive Study of Nursing Students," 132.

14 Fiorinelli et al, "Smartphone Distraction During Nursing Care: Systematic Literature Review," *Applied Nursing Research* 58 (2021): 151405.

15 Fiorinelli et al, "Smartphone Distraction During Nursing Care: Systematic Literature Review," 2.

16 Alameddine et al., "The Use of Smart Devices By Care Providers in Emergency Departments: Cross-Sectional Survey Design," *JMIR Mhealth Uhealth* 7, no. 6 (2019): 5. One phenomenon that emerges in multiple studies is that many more individuals report witnessing others being distracted by smartphones and committing errors than self-report being distracted and committing errors. Following this quotation, the authors note, "Interestingly, only 15 out of 93 respondents (16%) acknowledged that they did make an error or a near miss as a result of being distracted by their SDs" (ibid.).

17 McBride, "Nursing Performance and Mobile Phone Use: Are Nurses Aware of Their Performance Decrements?," *JMIR Hum Factors* 2, no. 1 (2015): 3. To be specific, rather than smartphones, this study refers to "personal communication device[s] ... defined as a wireless handheld device owned by an individual which can make and receive telephone calls or which provides a connection to the Internet via email, text messaging, videoconferencing, and social networking software. This definition includes cellular phones, mobile phones with app capabilities, and electronic tablet computers, but excludes desktop computers, pagers, or any company-provided device." D. McBride, S. LeVasseur, and D. Li, "Nursing Performance and Mobile Phone Use: Are Nurses Aware of Their Performance Decrements?," *JMIR Hum Factors* 2, no. 1 (2015): 2.

18 McBride, "Nursing Performance and Mobile Phone Use," 3.

19 McBride, "Nursing Performance and Mobile Phone Use," 3.

20 McBride, "Nursing Performance and Mobile Phone Use," 3.

21 Association of Perioperative Registered Nurses, "AORN Position Statement on Managing Distractions and Noise During Perioperative Patient Care." *AORN Journal* 111, no. 6 (2020): 675.

22 Association of Perioperative Registered Nurses, "AORN Position Statement on Managing Distractions and Noise During Perioperative Patient Care," 676.

23 American College of Surgeons (ACS) Committee on Perioperative Care, "Statement on Distractions in the Operating Room," *The Bulletin of the American College of Surgeons* 101, no. 10 (2016): 42–4.

24 ACS, "Statement on Distractions in the Operating Room," 44.

25 Quoting Michelle Feil, Distractions in the operating room. Patient Safety Advisory. June 2014. Available at: patientsafetyauthority.org/ADVISORIES/AdvisoryLibrary/2014/jun;11(2)/Pages/45.aspx. Accessed August 15, 2016.

26 ACS, "Statement on Distractions in the Operating Room," 42.

27 ACS, "Statement on Distractions in the Operating Room," 42–3.

28 ACS, "Statement on Distractions in the Operating Room," 42.

29 ACS, "Statement on Distractions in the Operating Room," 43.

30 Sihui Ma et al., "Persistence of Multitasking Distraction Following the Use of Smartphone-Based Clickers," *International Journal of Teaching and Learning in Higher Education* 32, no. 1 (2020): 64.

31 Simon Amez and Stijn Baert, "Smartphone Use and Academic Performance: A Literature Review," *International Journal of Educational Research* 103 (2020): 7.

32 Amez, "Smartphone Use and Academic Performance: A Literature Review," 3, emphasis added.

33 Amez, "Smartphone Use and Academic Performance: A Literature Review," 3.

34 Inyeop Kim et al., "Understanding Smartphone Usage in College Classrooms: A Long-Term Measurement Study," *Computers & Education* 141 (2019): 14.

35 Fritjof Sahlström et al., "Connected Youth, Connected Classrooms. Smartphone Use and Student and Teacher Participation During Plenary Teaching," *Learning, Culture and Social Interaction* 21 (2019).

36 Sahlström et al., "Connected Youth, Connected Classrooms. Smartphone Use and Student and Teacher Participation During Plenary Teaching," 328.

37 Sahlström et al., "Connected Youth, Connected Classrooms. Smartphone Use and Student and Teacher Participation During Plenary Teaching," 329.

38 The researchers put this as follows. "[W]e have selected as examples five cases from the collection of lessons, which best illustrate the different phone use patterns, and represents the observed variation in the data." Sahlström et al., "Connected Youth, Connected Classrooms. Smartphone Use and Student and Teacher Participation During Plenary Teaching," 313.

39 Sahlström et al., "Connected Youth, Connected Classrooms. Smartphone Use and Student and Teacher Participation During Plenary Teaching," 315; by "material," they mean data.

40 Sahlström et al., "Connected Youth, Connected Classrooms. Smartphone Use and Student and Teacher Participation During Plenary Teaching," 316.

41 Sahlström et al., "Connected Youth, Connected Classrooms. Smartphone Use and Student and Teacher Participation During Plenary Teaching," 315.

42 Sahlström et al., "Connected Youth, Connected Classrooms. Smartphone Use and Student and Teacher Participation During Plenary Teaching," 316.

43 Although they do not discuss meaningfulness explicitly, Strong and Higgs emphasize this general point about Borgmann's philosophy, but as a way of flagging what is insightful about Borgmann's theory of technology, the Device Paradigm: "[A]nd this is Borgmann's central insight, devices *split* means and ends into *mere means* and *mere ends*. . . . [focal] Things, in contrast, richly interweave means and ends, so that practices are experienced as good in their own right and useful too." Strong and Higgs, "Borgmann's Philosophy of Technology," 29, emphasis in original.

44 Thomas M. Alexander, *John Dewey's Theory of Art, Experience, and Nature* (Albany: State University of New York Press, 1987), 201, emphasis in original.

45 Alexander, *John Dewey's Theory of Art, Experience, and Nature*, 212, emphasis in original; quoting Dewey from *Art as Experience*, 55.

46 Dewey, *Art as Experience*, 56. Consider the following passage as well: "This consummation, moreover, does not wait in consciousness for the whole undertaking to be finished. It is anticipated throughout and is recurrently savored with special intensity." Dewey, *Art as Experience*, 55. We can be more specific, but the conclusion would be the same: "There are two kinds of means. One kind is external to that which is accomplished; the other kind is taken up into the consequences produced and remains immanent in them. There are ends which are merely welcome cessations and there are ends that are fulfillments of what went before . . . Such external or mere means, as we properly term them, are usually of such a sort that others can be substituted for them." Dewey, *Art as Experience*, 197.

47 On this general point, Hubert Dreyfus is following William Blattner. Cf. Dreyfus, "Audio Lectures on Heidegger's *Being and Time* (Philosophy 185)" (2007), Lectures 5 and 15. Cf. William Blattner, *Heidegger's "Being and Time": A Reader's Guide* (London: Continuum, 2006), 147–8. William Blattner, *Heidegger's Temporal Idealism* (Cambridge: Cambridge University Press, 1999), Chapter 2.

48 Cf. Sherry Turkle, *Reclaiming Conversation: The Power of Talk in a Digital Age* (New York: Penguin, 2015), 30.

49 Michelle A. Feil, "Distractions in the Operating Room," in *Distracted Doctoring: Returning to Patient-Centered Care in the Digital Age*, ed. Stephen Bertman and Peter J. Papadakos (Berlin: Springer, 2017), 151.

50 See Irwing Koch et al., "Cognitive Structure, Flexibility, and Plasticity in Human Multitasking—An Integrative Review of Dual-Task and Task-Switching Research," *Psychological Bulletin* 144, no. 6 (2018): 562, 564.

51 Koch, "Cognitive Structure, Flexibility, and Plasticity in Human Multitasking—an Integrative Review of Dual-Task and Task-Switching Research," 572; this is a description of the work in the following: E. Ruthruff et al., "How does practice reduce dual-task interference: Integration, automatization, or just stage-shortening?" *Psychological Research*, 70 (2006), 125–142.

52 Regarding the metaphor of a bottleneck, see Michael N. Tombu et al., "A Unified Attentional Bottleneck in the Human Brain," *PNAS* 108, no. 33 (2011).

53 Automaticity is discussed in the psychology research. Consider the following passage from Skaugset and her colleagues. "Multitasking, the simultaneous performance of two discrete tasks, can occur only when two tasks are automatic. Automatic tasks are those that are solidified in long-term memory through practice, learning, and repetition, almost subconsciously. Dually performed automatic tasks are more typically those that are practiced most frequently; for example, walking and talking. In contrast, nonautomatic tasks require conscious, deliberate attention and are limited to the capacity of working memory. The result is that simultaneous performance of nonautomatic multiple tasks is not possible." L. Melissa Skaugset et al., "Can You Multitask? Evidence and Limitations of Task Switching and Multitasking in Emergency Medicine," *Annals of Emergency Medicine* 68, no. 2 (2016): 191. Regarding "task automatization" and "task integration," see Koch, "Cognitive Structure, Flexibility, and Plasticity in Human Multitasking—an Integrative Review of Dual-Task and Task-Switching Research," 572.

54 Cf. Galit Wellner, "Multi-Attention and the Horcrux Logic: Justifications for Talking on the Cell Phone While Driving," *Techné: Research in Philosophy and Technology* 18, no. 1–2 (2014): 60.

55 Whether these are examples of dual-task performance or serial task-switching is unclear. At the macro level, which Wellner and Michelfelder are considering, such tasks are certainly happening at the same time, but what is happening at

the level of perception, response time, and so on, is unclear. It could very well be that in such cases one rapidly switches attention between driving and talking.

56 I am uncomfortable even hinting at distinctions between perception, cognition, and action. Note that drawing such distinctions is itself problematic from a Merleau-Pontean perspective.

57 Diane Michelfelder, "Driving While Beagleated," *Techné: Research in Philosophy and Technology* 18, no. 1–2 (2014): 124.

58 Michelfelder, "Driving While Beagleated," 124.

59 For example, Fried and her colleagues conducted a study that included "[o]ne hundred thirty-seven students, from two sections of General Psychology taught by the same instructor." They found that "the level of laptop use was significantly and negatively related to student learning ... The more students used their laptops in class, the lower their class performance." Carrie B. Fried, "In-Class Laptop Use and Its Effects on Student Learning," *Computers & Education* 50, no. 3 (2008): 908, 910. Also see Faria Sana et al., "Laptop Multitasking Hinders Classroom Learning for Both Users and Nearby Peers," *Computers & Education* 62 (2013).

60 I am channeling some basic points made by Merleau-Ponty. See Maurice Merleau-Ponty, *Phenomenology of Perception,* trans. Donald A. Landes (London and New York: Routledge, 2012), Introduction.

61 Robert Rosenberger, drawing upon the work of the phenomenologist Aaron Gurwitsch, has made this point about technology generally, calling this phenomenon *field composition:* "With the notion of 'field composition', I refer to ways that some relations to technology involve substantial reorganizations of the total field of our awareness." Robert Rosenberger, "The Phenomenological Case for Stricter Regulation of Cell Phones and Driving," *Techné: Research in Philosophy and Technology* (2014): 26.

62 I will quote Rosenberger below. I should point out that this general point has its source in Heidegger's claim that equipment withdraws while it is working; cf. Martin Heidegger, *Being and Time,* trans. John Macquarrie and Edward Robinson (Oxford: Blackwell Publishers Ltd, 1962), 99. A more recent source is Don Ihde's "embodiment relation." Cf. Don Ihde, *Technology and the Lifeworld: From Garden to Earth* (Bloomington and Indianapolis: Indiana University Press, 1990), 72–80.

63 Jane Vincent, *Emotion in the Social Practices of Mobile Phone Users* (Guildford: University of Surrey, 2011), 3.

64 Rosenberger, "The Phenomenological Case for Stricter Regulation of Cell Phones and Driving," 27.

65 Robert Rosenberger and Peter-Paul Verbeek, "A Postphenomenological Field Guide," in *Postphenomenological Investigations: Essays on Human–Technology Relations,* ed. Robert Rosenberger and Peter-Paul Verbeek (Lanham: Lexington Books, 2015), 25.

66 Dominant stability is to be contrasted with what Don Ihde calls multistability. Rosenberger glosses Ihde's concept of multistability in this way: "Multistability refers to a technology's capacity to hold different meanings for different users, and to be used for multiple purposes." Rosenberger, "The Phenomenological Case for Stricter Regulation of Cell Phones and Driving," 37.

67 Rosenberger, "The Phenomenological Case for Stricter Regulation of Cell Phones and Driving," 39–40.

68 Rosenberger draws this distinction. Cf. Rosenberger, "The Phenomenological Case for Stricter Regulation of Cell Phones and Driving," 35.

69 Tablets seem to be intermediate cases; whether they occupy an intimate place within one's life depends upon how one uses them.

70 P. Gill, A. Kamath, and T. S. Gill, "Distraction: An Assessment of Smartphone Usage in Health Care Work Settings," *Risk Management and Healthcare Policy* 5 (2012): 108.

71 L. Srivastava, "Mobile Phones and the Evolution of Social Behaviour," *Behaviour & Information Technology* 24, no. 2 (2005): 112–13. (Srivastava is the Head of Emerging Technology & Emerging Economies at the International Telecommunication Union's Standardization Bureau.)

72 Jingjing Jiang, "How Teens and Parents Navigate Screen Time and Device Distractions." *PEW Research Center* (August 22, 2018).

73 Cf. Jane Vincent, "Emotional Attachment and Mobile Phones." *Knowledge Technology and Policy* 19, no. 1 (2006): 39–44. Also see Jane Vincent "Emotion and Mobile Phones." In *Mobile Democracy: Communications in the 21st Century,* ed. Kristóf Nyíri (Vienna: Passagen Verlag, 2003).

74 Srivastava, "Mobile Phones and the Evolution of Social Behaviour," 113, emphasis added.

75 Nancy Cheever et al., "Out of Sight is Not Out of Mind: The Impact of Restricting Wireless Mobile Device Use on Anxiety Levels Among Low, Moderate and High Users," *Computers in Human Behavior* 37 (2014): 290.

76 Cheever, "Out of Sight is Not Out of Mind: The Impact of Restricting Wireless Mobile Device Use on Anxiety Levels Among Low, Moderate and High Users," 295.

77 Vincent writes: "Although the mobile phone is but one means of communication amongst a plethora of ICTs [information and communication technologies], there seems to be something that makes it appear more personal, more intimate than the fixed phone, the laptop, or the desktop computer. There is virtually nowhere you cannot take a mobile phone now. It may be that etiquette and courtesy, or regulations forbid its use in certain places (such as in places of worship, in most airplanes and so on), but even when this occurs the mobile phone is often still in a trouser or jacket pocket, handbag or briefcase, placed on silent or airplane mode and ready to be turned back on in an instant. The effect of this is to maintain a constant presence not only of the mobile phone itself but, more pertinently, of the communications, images and other personalised information that is sent, received and stored on it. At any moment this can be reached through the stimulation of the touch of the device, the thought of it, or the actual receipt of a communication from a third party." Vincent, *Emotion in the Social Practices of Mobile Phone Users*, 170.

78 Vincent, *Emotion in the Social Practices of Mobile Phone Users*, 136.

79 Vincent, *Emotion in the Social Practices of Mobile Phone Users*, 138–40.

80 Referring to a particular respondent, Vincent writes: "George could make contact with his family from his hotel room, but only with a voice call—and this was not a substitute for a late night text message, or the feeling that he could be instantly in contact using his familiar mobile with all its contacts and short cuts for communication, as well as the special ring tones for family members and other aspects of the phone he had personalised. For example, he kept the last text from many of his contact list and replied to that, rather than looking up their number." Vincent, *Emotion in the Social Practices of Mobile Phone Users*, 141.

81 Vincent, *Emotion in the Social Practices of Mobile Phone Users*, 141.

82 Jiang, "How Teens and Parents Navigate Screen Time and Device Distractions."

3　Developed Experience

1　We will encounter Borgmann making a version of this claim in Chapter 5.

2　Synonyms for "*an* experience" include "integral experience" and "complete experience." In the context of criticizing Dewey's metaphysics, Bernstein mentions the distinction between Dewey's "phenomenological and metaphysical strains." Richard J. Bernstein, "John Dewey's Metaphysics of Experience," *Journal of Philosophy* LVIII, no. 1 (1961): 5. Bernstein takes Dewey's metaphysics to be irreconcilable with his phenomenology. Cf. Bernstein, "John Dewey's Metaphysics of Experience," 5–8. Cf. Alexander, *John Dewey's Theory of Art, Experience, and Nature*, 65. Also see Roland Garrett, "Dewey's Struggle With the Ineffable," *Transactions of the Charles S. Peirce Society* 9, no. 2 (1973).

3　In the secondary literature, it is not uncommon to describe Dewey's "*an* experience" as "developed." Cf. Casey Haskins, "Dewey's *Art as Experience* in the Landscape of Twenty-First-century Aesthetics," in *The Oxford Handbook of Dewey*, ed. Steven Fesmire (New York: Oxford University Press, 2019), 445. Also see Steven Fesmire, *Dewey* (London and New York: Routledge, 2015), 191. Dewey himself uses the phrase (Cf. Dewey, *Art as Experience*, 37–43). Alexander writes, "The primary feature of *an* experience is that it is an affair of *temporal* development. Not only is there progression, but there is progressive integration which gathers the temporal phases together as belonging, relating to each other, sustaining and interacting with each other in a tensive, dramatic unity so that there is a cumulative sense of an overall event being accomplished or brought to completion." Alexander, *John Dewey's Theory of Art, Experience, and Nature*, 201, emphasis in original; also see 241.

4　I take "wan" from Martin Jay, *Songs of Experience: Modern American and European Variations on a Universal Theme* (Berkeley and Los Angeles: University of California Press, 2005), 43. (I owe thanks to Casey Haskins for recommending Jay's book.)

5　See Chapter 2 of Jay, *Songs of Experience*.

6　James defines this fallacy in his *Principles of Psychology* just after mentioning Locke and Hume. See William James, *The Principles of Psychology* (New York: Henry Holt & Co., 1890), 194 ff.

7　Alexander, *John Dewey's Theory of Art, Experience, and Nature*, 72, emphasis in original.

8　Cf. Merleau-Ponty, *Phenomenology of Perception*, Introduction.

9   Note, however, that this critique is limited by just what one is conscious of. If representations (say) are defined as things of which we are not conscious, then this critique has no leverage.

10   James, *The Principles of Psychology*, 196.

11   Alexander, *John Dewey's Theory of Art, Experience, and Nature*, 197.

12   Alexander, *John Dewey's Theory of Art, Experience, and Nature*, 57.

13   Dewey, *Art as Experience*, 44–5.

14   Dewey, *Art as Experience*, 151.

15   Dewey, *Art as Experience*, 44.

16   Dewey, *Art as Experience*, 44.

17   I am attempting to take these straightforward ideas on board without delving into Dewey's metaphysics, and without explicitly invoking a Merleau-Pontean conception of motor intentionality. An existential phenomenologist may be concerned that certain kinds of awareness may conflict with absorbed engagement (being in-flow, in a groove). Although it is true that *perceptually scrutinizing* aspects of an activity can disrupt absorbed engagement, this is not the only sense of awareness available. I am interested in forms of awareness and experiential quality that may be consistent with absorbed engagement. Can we work toward understanding our awareness of what Dewey calls experiential phases and their relations as a component of being keyed-in to an activity? Relevant to these issues is my discussion of motor intentionality and the awareness needed to grasp a groove in Chapters 3 and 4 of Roholt, *Groove: A Phenomenology of Rhythmic Nuance* (New York and London: Bloomsbury Academic, 2014).

18   I am aware of the meaning of "situation" in Dewey's metaphysics; I am attempting to use the term suggestively without directly engaging his metaphysics.

19   Alexander stresses this dimension: "[I]t is not enough simply to assert that because experience has phases of doing and undergoing it thereby has structure. These phases must be *related* to each other or coordinated, and this relation itself must be recognized before meaning can arise." Alexander, *John Dewey's Theory of Art, Experience, and Nature*, 127, emphasis in original.

20   Dewey, *Art as Experience*, 36.

21   Dewey, *Art as Experience*, 40, emphasis in original.

22 Roholt, *Groove*, 113.

23 Dewey, *Art as Experience*, 44, emphasis added.

24 Dewey, *Art as Experience*, 18.

25 Dewey, *Art as Experience*, 18.

26 Dewey, *Art as Experience*, 18.

27 Dewey, *Art as Experience*, 18.

28 Dewey, *Art as Experience*, 18.

29 Fesmire, *Dewey*, 193.

30 Dewey, *Art as Experience*, 42–3.

31 Dewey, *Art as Experience*, 52, emphasis in original.

32 Dewey, *Art as Experience*, 53, emphasis in original. Consider this quotation: "Identification nods and passes on. Or it defines a passing moment in isolation, it marks a dead spot in experience that is merely filled in. The extent to which the process of living in any day or hour is reduced to labeling situations, events, and objects as 'so-and-so' in mere succession marks the cessation of a life that is a conscious experience. Continuities realized in an individual, discrete, form are the essence ot the latter." Dewey, *Art as Experience*, 25.

33 Dewey, *Art as Experience*, 43.

34 Dewey, *Art as Experience*, 147.

35 Dewey, *Art as Experience*, 43–4.

36 Dewey, *Art as Experience*, 13–14.

37 Note that this is true even if the interview is not a developed experience but instead consists of disjointed stock questions and answers.

38 Dewey, *Art as Experience*, 14, emphasis added.

39 Dewey, *Art as Experience*, 39.

40 John Dewey, *Logic: The Theory of Inquiry* (New York: Henry Holt and Company, 1938), 175–6, emphasis in original.

41 Dewey, *Art as Experience*, 35, emphasis in original.

42 Dewey, *Art as Experience*, 36, emphasis in original.

43 Cf. Alexander, *John Dewey's Theory of Art, Experience, and Nature*, 200.

44 Alexander, *John Dewey's Theory of Art, Experience, and Nature*, 200.

45 Alexander, *John Dewey's Theory of Art, Experience, and Nature*, 211, emphasis in original.

46 Cf. Dewey, *Art as Experience*, 17, 23, 137. Also see John Dewey, *Experience and Nature* (London: George Allen & Unwin, Ltd, 1929), 269.

47 Dewey, *Art as Experience*, 35, emphasis added. Here is the full quotation: "A piece of work is finished in a way that is satisfactory; a problem receives its solution; a game is played through; a situation, whether that of eating a meal, playing a game of chess, carrying on a conversation, writing a book, or taking part in a political campaign, is so rounded out that its close is a consummation and not a cessation."

48 Richard J. Bernstein, *John Dewey* (New York: Washington Square Press, 1966), 96.

49 Dewey, *Art as Experience*, 36.

50 Pervasive qualities "can unify a situation" or context. Bernstein, "John Dewey's Metaphysics of Experience," 7.

51 Alexander, *John Dewey's Theory of Art, Experience, and Nature*, 104.

52 John J. Stuhr, "Dewey's Notion of Qualitative Experience," *Transactions of the Charles S. Peirce Society* 15, no. 1 (1979): 74.

53 Dewey, *Logic*, 69, emphasis in original.

54 Dewey, *Logic*, 70.

55 Cf. Fesmire, *Dewey*, 193.

56 Dewey, *Art as Experience*, 38, emphasis in original.

57 Bernstein, "John Dewey's Metaphysics of Experience," 8, emphasis in original. In fact, it is this richly qualitative account of developed experience that enables Dewey to ground his aesthetic theory in developed experience generally: "I have tried to show in these chapters that the esthetic is no intruder in experience from without . . . it is the clarified and intensified development of traits that belong to every normally complete experience [i.e., *an* experience]." Dewey, *Art as Experience*, 46.

58 Alexander, *John Dewey's Theory of Art, Experience, and Nature*, 185, emphasis in original.

59 Cf. Alexander, *John Dewey's Theory of Art, Experience, and Nature*, 250.

60 Dewey, *Logic: The Theory of Inquiry*, 70, emphasis in original.

61 Regarding a pervasive quality's uniqueness, see Dewey, *Logic: The Theory of Inquiry*, 68–70.

62 See W. E. Kennick, "Art and the Ineffable," *Journal of Philosophy* 58, no. 12 (1961).

63 Ludwig Wittgenstein, *The Blue and Brown Books* (Oxford: Blackwell, 1998[1933–1935]).

64 Wittgenstein, *The Blue and Brown Books*, 181.

65 Wittgenstein, *The Blue and Brown Books*, 181.

66 Dewey, *Art as Experience*, 35.

67 Cf. Dewey, *Art as Experience*, 55, 25.

68 Dewey, *Art as Experience*, 44.

69 Alexander, *John Dewey's Theory of Art, Experience, and Nature*, 211, emphasis in original.

70 Dewey, *Art as Experience*, 52.

71 R. G. Collingwood, *The Principles of Art* (New York: Oxford University Press, 1958), 140–1.

72 Dewey, *Art as Experience*, 36

73 Dewey, *Art as Experience*, 36.

74 Dewey, *Art as Experience*, 36.

4 Meaning in Life

1 Thaddeus Metz, *Meaning in Life: An Analytic Study* (New York: Oxford University Press, 2013), 182.

2 Susan Wolf, *Meaning in Life and Why It Matters* (Princeton: Princeton University Press, 2010), 109.

3 A useful, basic formulation of hedonism is what Fred Feldman calls Default Hedonism. Although, in order for this conception to be helpful here, we would have to ignore what he says in the same chapter about happiness. See Fred Feldman, *Pleasure and the Good Life* (Oxford and New York: Oxford University Press, 2004), Chapter 2.

4 Cf. Wolf, *Meaning in Life and Why It Matters*, 8.

5 Wolf, *Meaning in Life and Why It Matters*, 36–7.

6 Cf. Wolf, *Meaning in Life and Why It Matters*, 29–30.

7 Wolf, *Meaning in Life and Why It Matters*, 113. There are clearly many pleasures that are not cases of fulfillment: "Riding a roller coaster, meeting a movie star, eating a hot fudge sundae, finding a great dress on sale." Wolf, *Meaning in Life and Why It Matters*, 114. It may be clearer to conceive of pleasure as one kind of feeling or sensation, while conceiving of the various causes of pleasure that Wolf mentions as "pleasant things." Cf. Feldman, *Pleasure and the Good Life*, 23 and 29.

8 Wolf, *Meaning in Life and Why It Matters*, 112.

9 Cf. Wolf, *Meaning in Life and Why It Matters*, 112.

10 Wolf, *Meaning in Life and Why It Matters*, 114.

11 See Wolf, *Meaning in Life and Why It Matters*, 45. Also see Susan Wolf, "Meaning in Life: Meeting the Challenges," *Foundations of Science* 21, no. 2 (2016): 281–2.

12 Wolf, *Meaning in Life and Why It Matters*, 130–1.

13 I am referring to a passage in which Wolf is responding to a commentary by Arnold Burms: "[T]hough I find promising Burms' suggestion that we approach the concept of objectivity in a way that does not identify it with neutrality or impersonalism, many difficulties to the idea remain." Wolf, "Meaning in Life: Meeting the Challenges," 282.

14 Wolf, *Meaning in Life and Why It Matters*, 45.

15 Wolf, *Meaning in Life and Why It Matters*, 37.

16 Wolf, *Meaning in Life and Why It Matters*, 37.

17 See "The Meanings of Lives," in *Introduction to Philosophy: Classical and Contemporary Readings*, ed. John Perry, Michael Bratman, and John Martin Fischer (New York: Oxford University Press, 2016), 62–73.

18 In her 2014 article, "Meaningfulness: A Third Dimension of the Good Life," Wolf describes the objectivity at issue in this way: "To acknowledge that a person may be mistaken about what has value, and that finding something valuable doesn't necessarily make it so, is hardly to commit oneself to a view that value is a nonnatural property, or that it is built into 'the fabric of the universe'. Nor does believing that one can be mistaken about value, or even

that everyone can be mistaken about value, imply that values might even in principle be independent of human (or other conscious beings') needs and capacities." See Susan Wolf, "Meaningfulness: A Third Dimension of the Good Life," *Foundations of Science* 21, no. 2 (2014): 265.

19 Wolf, *Meaning in Life and Why It Matters*, 128, emphasis in original.

20 Wolf, *Meaning in Life and Why It Matters*, 44. "The kind of objectivity that seems necessary for meaning is a kind that implies that one can be mistaken about value. A person's liking something or thinking it to be valuable doesn't make it so (nor does her disliking something or thinking it not to be valuable make that so)." Wolf, *Meaning in Life and Why It Matters*, 131.

21 Wolf, *Meaning in Life and Why It Matters*, 37.

22 Wolf, *Meaning in Life and Why It Matters*, 44–5.

23 Wolf, *Meaning in Life and Why It Matters*, 24.

24 Cf. Wolf, *Meaning in Life and Why It Matters*, 23.

25 Wolf, *Meaning in Life and Why It Matters*, 24.

26 Cf. Wolf, *Meaning in Life and Why It Matters*, 9, 11.

27 Wolf, *Meaning in Life and Why It Matters*, 22.

28 Wolf, *Meaning in Life and Why It Matters*, 14.

29 Wolf, *Meaning in Life and Why It Matters*, 4, 14.

30 I would like to flag a concern that existential phenomenologists will have with the term "subjective." I am using "subjective" in order to retain a connection to Wolf's theory. One reason existential phenomenologists avoid this term is due to its suggestion of a private, inner realm of experience. As my preference for "being gripped" here suggests, we can effectively characterize Wolf's subjective condition (subjective fulfillment) without reference to a private, inner realm.

31 Alexander, *John Dewey's Theory of Art, Experience, and Nature*, 200, 239.

32 Dewey, *Art as Experience*, 36.

33 Wolf mentions running as potentially meaningful; cf. Wolf, *Meaning in Life and Why It Matters*, 37.

34 Strong and Higgs, "Borgmann's Philosophy of Technology," 23.

35 Wolf, *Meaning in Life and Why It Matters*, 9–10.

5 Focal Things and Practices

1   While Borgmann does not use terms such as "meaningful" or "worthwhile," he raises the related notion of *significance*, referring to focal things and practices as "ultimately significant." Albert Borgmann, *Technology and the Character of Contemporary Life*, 209. Relatedly, he remarks, "'significance' is nothing but the highest generic term for things and practices that stand out in their own right." Ibid., 103. Borgmann also refers to focal practices as "guardians of the concrete things and events that finally matter." Ibid., 209. (The "things" at issue here are, of course, focal things.) Cf. 80, 188, 214, 218. Cf. David Strong and Eric Higgs, "Borgmann's Philosophy of Technology," in *Technology and the Good Life?*, ed. Eric Higgs, Andrew Light, and David Strong (Chicago and London: University of Chicago Press, 2000), 26, 36. Cf. Lawrence Haworth, "Focal Things and Practices," in *Technology and the Good Life?*, 59–60.

2   Albert Borgmann, *Technology and the Character of Contemporary Life*, 219. On 219, he also refers to the features of focal things and practices as "a set of traits that focal things and practices exhibit for the most part."

3   Borgmann, *Technology and the Character of Contemporary Life*, 135. As we have just seen, "machinery," for Borgmann, refers to a device's inner-workings, its mechanisms. For precisely what he means by "commodity," see Borgmann, *Technology and the Character of Contemporary Life*, 259 n.5.

4   Recall, in Chapter 2, I said that we cannot cash out meaningfulness through a means/end analysis. This is where the claim takes root in Borgmann.

5   Borgmann, *Technology and the Character of Contemporary Life*, 81.

6   Strictly speaking, this is a reference to a Heideggerian subworld, such as the academic world, the drug culture, the art world, and so on.

7   Borgmann, *Technology and the Character of Contemporary Life*, 80.

8   Strong and Higgs, "Borgmann's Philosophy of Technology," 23.

9   Borgmann, *Technology and the Character of Contemporary Life*, 41.

10   Borgmann, *Technology and the Character of Contemporary Life*, 205.

11   Borgmann, *Technology and the Character of Contemporary Life*, 197.

12   With technological progress, obtaining music becomes easier and easier. When we used to go buy vinyl records at record stores, we were connected to an aspect of a musical community that we are now disconnected from,

viz., record store employees. If you were lucky enough to live in a town where these people were knowledgable (as I was), shopping for records involved enriching, informative social interactions. Sadly, recommending music is now too often conducted by algorithm.

13 Albert Borgmann, "Reply to My Critics," in *Technology and the Good Life?*, 350–1.

14 Strong and Higgs, "Borgmann's Philosophy of Technology," 22–3.

15 Note that we are in the territory of what Maurice Merleau-Ponty calls motor intentionality. See Merleau-Ponty, *Phenomenology of Perception*, 139-48.

16 Cf. Strong and Higgs, "Borgmann's Philosophy of Technology," 22.

17 George Sturt, *The Wheelwright's Shop* (Cambridge: Cambridge University Press, 1923).

18 Strong and Higgs take *the objects made* (wagons, for example) to be the focal things.

19 Sturt, *The Wheelwright's Shop*, 24.

20 With this use of "embody," I am gesturing at Don Ihde. See his *Technology and the Lifeworld: From Garden to Earth* (Bloomington and Indianapolis: Indiana University Press, 1990).

21 Hubert Dreyfus and Sean D. Kelly, *All Things Shining: Reading the Western Classics to Find Meaning in a Secular Age* (New York: Free Press, 2011), 208.

22 Borgmann, *Technology and the Character of Contemporary Life*, 42.

23 Dreyfus and Kelly, *All Things Shining*, 207.

24 Dreyfus and Kelly, *All Things Shining*, 207.

25 Albert Borgmann, *Crossing the Postmodern Divide*.

26 Borgmann, *Technology and the Character of Contemporary Life*, 216.

27 Cf. Martin Heidegger, "The Thing," in *Poetry, Language, Thought* (New York: Harper & Row, 1971). Martin Heidegger, "On the Origin of the Work of Art," in *Poetry, Language, Thought* (New York: Harper & Row, 1971).

28 Cf. Borgmann, *Technology and the Character of Contemporary Life*, 197.

29 Borgmann, *Technology and the Character of Contemporary Life*, 199. Cf. Hubert Dreyfus, "Heidegger on Gaining a Free Relation to Technology," in *Heidegger Reexamined, Volume 3: Art, Poetry, and Technology*, ed. Hubert Dreyfus and Mark Wrathall (New York and London: Routledge, 2002), 171.

30 Borgmann, *Technology and the Character of Contemporary Life*, 198.

31 Borgmann, *Technology and the Character of Contemporary Life*, 198.

32 Cf. Borgmann, *Technology and the Character of Contemporary Life*, 218.

33 Strong and Higgs, "Borgmann's Philosophy of Technology," 23.

34 Borgmann, *Technology and the Character of Contemporary Life*, 219.

35 Daniel C. Dennett, "Information, Technology, and the Virtue of Ignorance," *Daedalus* 115 (1986): 143.

36 Charles Taylor, *Sources of the Self: The Making of the Modern Identity* (Cambridge, MA: Harvard University Press, 1989), 204.

37 Borgmann, *Technology and the Character of Contemporary Life*, 5.

38 Borgmann, *Technology and the Character of Contemporary Life*, 3.

39 Borgmann, *Technology and the Character of Contemporary Life*, 207.

40 Borgmann, *Technology and the Character of Contemporary Life*, 209.

41 "The technological view of a meal reveals an aggregate of tastes, textures, and nutritive features. They alone retain stable significance. How they come to be constituted and placed on the table is determined by the requirements of instantaneity, ubiquity, safety, and ease." Borgmann, *Technology and the Character of Contemporary Life*, 192.

42 "Countering technology through a practice is to take account of our susceptibility to technological distraction …" Borgmann, *Technology and the Character of Contemporary Life*, 210.

43 Borgmann, *Technology and the Character of Contemporary Life*, 119.

44 Martin Heidegger, "The Question Concerning Technology," in *The Question Concerning Technology, and Other Essays* (Harper & Row), (1977), 23.

45 Dreyfus, "Heidegger on Gaining a Free Relation to Technology," 166, emphasis in original.

46 Consider productivity movements such as "Getting Things Done."

47 Borgmann, *Technology and the Character of Contemporary Life*, 209.

48 Borgmann, *Technology and the Character of Contemporary Life*, 192.

49 Lawrence Haworth, "Focal Things and Focal Practices," in *Technology and the Good Life?*, ed. Eric Higgs, Andrew Light, and David Strong (Chicago and London: University of Chicago Press, 2000), 68.

50 Haworth, "Focal Things and Focal Practices," 68.

51 Borgmann, *Technology and the Character of Contemporary Life*, 80.

52 Strong and Higgs, "Borgmann's Philosophy of Technology," 22.

53 Haworth, "Focal Things and Focal Practices," 59.

54 Haworth uses the term "value," as does Wolf. Borgmann, some of his other commentators, and other existential phenomenologists, avoid the term. I employ the term here for the purpose of exploring connections to Wolf. As with my use of "subjective," my use of "value" could be eliminated; I often use the more uncontroversial "worthwhile" in place of "valuable." (In addition, consider Borgmann's "significant.") If I were to directly probe such conflicts between philosophical traditions, this would become a different kind of book. My strategy in this book is, instead, to ground my maneuvers in plain descriptions and concrete examples in order to show that I am not relying on problematic uses of such terms. I leave it to readers to decide whether I have managed this effectively.

55 Haworth, "Focal Things and Focal Practices," 64–5.

56 Haworth, "Focal Things and Focal Practices," 62.

57 Wolf, *Meaning in Life and Why It Matters*, 129, emphasis in original.

58 Borgmann, *Technology and the Character of Contemporary Life*, 207 (Borgmann is quoting Alasdair MacIntyre).

59 We can find fascinating support for this phenomenon in Dreyfus and Kelly's *All Things Shining*. They discuss the way in which certain situations can prop one up, and draw-out of one remarkable acts. These situations seem to be essentially social (regarding the social, communal aspect of this phenomenon, see Dreyfus and Kelly, *All Things Shining*, 204–05). Such situations have a kind of power, which Dreyfus and Kelly refer to as *physis*, a "whooshing-up." In these contexts, a person can "shine." Dreyfus and Kelly connect this phenomenon directly to meaningfulness. In the following passage, they discuss their interpretation of this phenomenon in Homer. "The most important things, the most real things in Homer's world, well up and take us over, hold us for a while, and then, finally, let us go. If we had to translate Homer's word *physis*, then whooshing is about as close as we can get. What there really is, for Homer, is whooshing up: the whooshing up of shining Achilles in the midst of battle.... And whooshing up is what happens in the context of the great moment in contemporary sport as well. When something whooshes up it focuses and organizes everything around it. The great athlete in the midst of the play rises up and shines." Dreyfus and Kelly, *All Things Shining*, 200–01.

60 Roholt, *Groove*, 137; cf. 120–2.

61 Borgmann, *Crossing the Postmodern Divide*, 106.

62 Wolf discusses sociality but approaches it from a different direction. Cf. Wolf, *Meaning in Life and Why It Matters*, 28–30.

63 Dreyfus and Kelly, *All Things Shining*, 193.

64 Strong and Higgs, "Borgmann's Philosophy of Technology," 24. The context of the following passage by Borgmann is a consideration of virtual golf vs. ordinary golf. "But what a reduced experience this is [virtual golf] compared with the real thing where mother and son share a time and a place that disclose the world to them and one to the other. In the latter case rising together, driving from home to the golf course, seeing the sun come up, feeling pride and gratitude to be citizens of this town and members of the golfing community—all this evaporates in virtual golf." Borgmann, "Reply to My Critics," 350.

65 One reason I employ "paraphernalia" is for its resonance with Heidegger's "*Zeug*." Cf. Heidegger, *Being and Time*, 97, n. 1. Cf. Blattner's use of "paraphernalia" in *Heidegger's* Being and Time, Chapter 3, §5. More practically, I do not use "instruments" because it would clash intolerably with our discussion of "musical instruments," which are focal things not "technological instruments," in Borgmann's sense. To be clear, in my terminology, musical instruments are not technological paraphernalia.

66 Borgmann, *Technology and the Character of Contemporary Life*, 221; italics are added to flag my alteration of "instruments" to "paraphernalia."

67 Borgmann, *Technology and the Character of Contemporary Life*, 288 n. 12; cf. 289 n. 23.

68 Hubert Dreyfus and Charles Spinosa, "Highway Bridges and Feasts: Heidegger and Borgmann on How to Affirm Technology," in *Heidegger Reexamined. Volume 3: Art, Poetry, and Technology*, ed. Hubert Dreyfus and Mark Wrathall (New York and London: Routledge, 2002), 185. Following Borgmann, they use the term "instrument."

69 Borgmann, *Technology and the Character of Contemporary Life*, 221.

70 Borgmann, *Technology and the Character of Contemporary Life*, 221.

71 Strong and Higgs, "Borgmann's Philosophy of Technology," 32.

72 Borgmann, *Technology and the Character of Contemporary Life*, 5.

73 Borgmann, *Technology and the Character of Contemporary Life*, 211.

74 Borgmann, *Technology and the Character of Contemporary Life*, 41–2, emphasis in original..

75 Strong and Higgs, "Borgmann's Philosophy of Technology," 23, emphasis in original.

76 As Erin Napier would put it.

77 Borgmann, *Technology and the Character of Contemporary Life*, 214; cf. 195.

78 See Borgmann, *Technology and the Character of Contemporary Life*, 202. Also see David Strong, *Crazy Mountains* (Albany: State University of New York Press, 1995), 200.

79 David Strong, "Philosophy in the Service of Things," in *Technology and the Good Life?*, ed. Eric Higgs, Andrew Light, David Strong (Chicago: The University of Chicago Press, 2000), 329. Cf. Strong, *Crazy Mountains*, 67–70.

80 Hubert Dreyfus, *Being-in-the-world: A Commentary on Heidegger's "Being and Time," Division I.* (Cambridge, MA: MIT Press, 1991), 23.

81 Borgmann, *Technology and the Character of Contemporary Life*, 42.

82 Strong and Higgs, "Borgmann's Philosophy of Technology," 23–4.

83 Strong and Higgs, "Borgmann's Philosophy of Technology," 22.

84 Borgmann, *Technology and the Character of Contemporary Life*, 214.

85 Strong and Higgs, "Borgmann's Philosophy of Technology," 23.

86 Borgmann, *Technology and the Character of Contemporary Life*, 5.

87 Cf. Wolf, *Meaning in Life and Why It Matters*, 127, 36–7, 123, 50, 29–30. Incidentally, there is no indication that Wolf has read Borgmann, and it is unlikely that she has, since she is working in a very different philosophical tradition—not merely different subfields but different traditions: Wolf is an analytic philosopher, and Borgmann is an existential phenomenologist.

88 Wolf, *Meaning in Life and Why It Matters*, 45, emphasis added.

89 Wolf, "Meaningfulness: A Third Dimension of the Good Life," 265, emphasis in original.

90 Borgmann, *Technology and the Character of Contemporary Life*, 209.

91 Wolf, *Meaning in Life and Why It Matters*, 37.

92 Wolf, *Meaning in Life and Why It Matters*, 42.

93 Wolf, "Meaningfulness: A Third Dimension of the Good Life," 261.

94 Wolf, "Meaningfulness: A Third Dimension of the Good Life," 262.

95 Cf. Borgmann, *Technology and the Character of Contemporary Life*, 44–5.

96 Dreyfus and Kelly, *All Things Shining*, 208–09.

97 Haworth, "Focal Things and Focal Practices," 55.

98 Borgmann, *Technology and the Character of Contemporary Life*, 42.

99 Wolf, *Meaning in Life and Why It Matters*, 9.

100 It becomes clear in other contexts that "endlessly" is not doing important work in Wolf's claim about the worthlessness of crosswords.

101 Wolf, *Meaning in Life and Why It Matters*, 130.

102 *Wordplay*. Directed by Patrick Creadon. IFC Films, 2006.

103 In addition to the tournament, the convention's website says, "Evening games, puzzles, and entertainments allow solvers to meet each other in a relaxed and entertaining atmosphere." Available at: https://www.crosswordtournament.com

104 *Wordplay*. These quotations occur at approximately 48:00. The quotation below occurs at approximately 14:00.

105 Wolf, *Meaning in Life and Why It Matters*, 16.

106 Wolf, *Meaning in Life and Why It Matters*, 14.

107 See Haworth's synthetic model of focal practices. Haworth, "Focal Things and Focal Practices," 63 ff.

108 Wolf, *Meaning in Life and Why It Matters*, 26.

109 Wolf, *Meaning in Life and Why It Matters*, 127.

110 Borgmann, *Technology and the Character of Contemporary Life*, 209.

111 If one were to develop this point in relation to Borgmann's philosophy, it would be worth taking into account precisely what Borgmann means by "commodity." Cf. Borgmann, *Technology and the Character of Contemporary Life*, 259 n.5.

112 I am reminded of Ken Bain's discussion of "strategic learning" in Bain, *What the Best College Teachers Do* (Cambridge, MA, and London: Harvard University Press, 2004). Bain's preference is for what he calls "deep learning."

113 Borgmann, *Technology and the Character of Contemporary Life*, 211.

114 Borgmann, *Technology and the Character of Contemporary Life*, 4.

115 Dewey, *Art as Experience*, 35.

6 Identity-Work

1 Heidegger's recently published Black Notebooks have revealed the depth of his anti-Semitism. See *Heidegger's Black Notebooks: Responses to Anti-Semitism*, ed. Mitchell, Andrew J., and Peter Trawny (New York: Columbia University Press, 2017). I believe that anyone writing about or teaching Heidegger must be vigilant for aspects of his philosophy that may serve as building blocks of anti-Semitism, and call out these aspects. The ideas I draw upon here do not seem to be such building blocks.

2 One can engage with seminars, colloquia, "Philosophy for Lunch" sessions, and so on, as part of the focal practice I am describing, but many people do not. Rather than approaching a seminar as a potentially meaningful event, some significant percentage of participants approach a seminar as a means to an end, whether the end is a final grade or the satisfaction of a program requirement. I suspect that it is even possible to approach a seminar with an objective to learn in a serious manner, what Ken Bain calls "deep learning," without opening oneself up to the possibility that the activity could generate meaning in one's life. Regarding deep learning, see Ken Bain, *What the Best College Teachers Do.*

3 For some empirical evidence that smartphone-use is contagious, see Julia A. Finkel and Daniel J. Kruger, "Is Cell Phone Use Socially Contagious?," *Human Ethology Bulletin* 27, no. 1–2 (2012).

4 Of course, there are other activities that contribute to shaping this part of Emma's identity. For example, she discusses philosophical ideas with other students outside of the classroom, she reads and writes about philosophy, she will likely visit office hours to have conversations with professors, she attends extra-curricular philosophy events, and so on.

5 Consider these passages on self-creation by Nietzsche and then Sartre: "We, however, want to become who we are—human beings who are new, unique, incomparable, who give themselves laws, who create themselves!" Friedrich Nietzsche, *The Gay Science*, trans. Josefine Nauckhoff (Cambridge: Cambridge University Press, 2001), §335. Sartre: "The doctrine I am presenting is the very opposite of quietism, since it declares, 'There is no reality except in action'. Moreover, it goes further, since it adds, 'Man is nothing else than his plan; he exists only to the extent that he fulfills himself; he is therefore nothing else than the ensemble of his acts, nothing else than his life." Jean-Paul Sartre, "Existentialism is a Humanism," in *Existentialism: Basic Writings*, ed. Charles Guignon and Derk Pereboom (Indianapolis: Hackett, 2001), 300. ¶ In discussing Heidegger, William Blattner writes the following about his (Blattner's) use of the term, "identity": "We care about our lives, our being is an issue for us. We constantly confront the question, or issue, Who am I? (To simplify my formulations, I will refer to this question as 'the question of identity'.) To confront the question of identity is not to brood over one's Identity. Brooding self-questioning is one way to live, but by no means common. We confront the question of identity not by reflecting on ourselves, but rather simply by living a human life. To live a life is to answer the question of identity." Blattner, *Heidegger's "Being and Time": A Reader's Guide*, 37.

6   Heidegger, *Being and Time*, 67.

7   Dreyfus, *Being-in-the-world: A Commentary on Heidegger's "Being and Time," Division I*, 23. There is a more common notion of the self that we are leaving behind here—the Cartesian conception. Heidegger maintains that the self is not a self-sufficient subject. It is instructive to note that to translate Dasein as "subject" would be misleading, due to the Cartesian baggage of the term. As Dreyfus writes, "The challenge is to do justice to the fact that Dasein names beings like you and me, while at the same time preserving the strategy of *Being and Time*, which is to reverse the Cartesian tradition by making the individual subject somehow dependent upon shared social practices." Dreyfus, *Being-in-the-world: A Commentary on Heidegger's "Being and Time," Division I*, 14.

8   Although I will use the term "role" for simplicity's sake, characterizing a for-the-sake-of-which as a role is imprecise, because the meaning of "role" is not sufficiently holistic; a role is problematically context-free (see Dreyfus 1991a, 95). It is acceptable to use "role" as long as we keep in mind that Heidegger's for-the-sake-of-which is holistic. Another way to cash out "for-the-sake-of-which" is as the "final point" of some number of actions. Cf. Taylor Carman, *Heidegger's Analytic: Interpretation, Discourse, and Authenticity* (Cambridge: Cambridge University Press, 2003), 133 n. 63. Cf. Dreyfus, *Being-in-the-world: A Commentary on Heidegger's "Being and Time," Division I*, 92. ¶ Regarding the multiplicity of for-the-sake-of-whichs, Blattner writes, "*Dasein* is never just one for-the-sake-of-which, but rather several or many of them at once. Jones is a simultaneous interpreter, a loyal sister, a conscientious employee, etc." William Blattner, "Existence and Self-Understanding in 'Being and Time," in *Heidegger Reexamined,*

Vol. 1, ed. Hubert Dreyfus and Mark Wrathall (New York: Routledge, 2002), 185 n. 2.

9   Dreyfus, *Being-in-the-world: A Commentary on Heidegger's "Being and Time," Division I*, 95.

10 Dreyfus, *Being-in-the-world: A Commentary on Heidegger's "Being and Time," Division I*, 96. Dreyfus continues: "And each practice is connected with a lot of equipment for practicing it. *Dasein* inhabits or dwells in these practices and their appropriate equipment; in fact *Dasein* takes a stand on its being by being a more or less integrated subpattern of social practices." Dreyfus, *Being-in-the-world: A Commentary on Heidegger's "Being and Time," Division I*, 96.

11 Robert Nozick, *The Examined Life: Philosophical Meditations* (New York: Touchstone, 1989), 303.

12 A more thorough examination of identity and Dasein would lead us to a consideration of authenticity.

13 "According to Heidegger, to explain everyday transparent coping we do not need to introduce a mental representation of a goal at all. Activity can be purposive without the actor having in mind a purpose." Dreyfus, *Being-in-the-world: A Commentary on Heidegger's "Being and Time," Division I*, 93.

14 As I said in 2.3, this potential value of a classroom context (i.e., the fact that it is a context in which one can engage in identity-work) falls through the cracks of the kind of means/ends analysis we find in the education studies described in 2.2.

15 Dreyfus refers to what I am calling a microcosm as a mode. "Such worlds as the business world, the child's world, and the world of mathematics, are 'modes' of the total system of equipment and practices that Heidegger calls the world." Dreyfus, *Being-in-the-world: A Commentary on Heidegger's "Being and Time," Division I*, 90. Dreyfus also uses the term "subworld." Dreyfus, *Being-in-the-world: A Commentary on Heidegger's "Being and Time," Division I*, 91.

16 Dreyfus, *Being-in-the-world: A Commentary on Heidegger's "Being and Time," Division I*, 92.

17 Dreyfus, *Being-in-the-world: A Commentary on Heidegger's "Being and Time," Division I*, 348 n.5.

18 "The phenomenological assertion that 'Dasein is essentially Being-with' has an existential-ontological meaning. It does not seek to establish ontically that factically I am not present-at-hand alone, and that Others of my kind occur." Heidegger, *Being and Time*, 156.

19 It is noteworthy that Heidegger takes being-with to be as foundational as being-in-the-world. Being-with is equiprimordial with being-in-the-world. Cf. Heidegger, *Being and Time*, 149–50. Theodore Schatzki makes the point straightforwardly: "Human existence is essentially being-in-the-world. It is equally essentially being-with." Theodore Schatzski, "Early Heidegger on Sociality," in *A Companion to Heidegger*, ed. Hubert Dreyfus and Mark Wrathall (Malden, MA: Blackwell Publishing, 2005), 233. Elsewhere, Schatzki elaborates as follows: "Heidegger's object of analysis is individual existence, but his analysis construes sociality as part of the essence of this existence." Theodore Schatzski, "Being, the Clearing, and Realism," in *Heidegger Reexamined, Volume 2: Truth, Realism, and the History of Being*, ed. Hubert Dreyfus and Mark Wrathall (New York: Routledge, 2002), 184.

20 Blattner, *Heidegger's Temporal Idealism*, 50 n.31. Being-with is ontological, while the particular roles we have been discussing are ontic. Cf. Dreyfus, *Being-in-the-world: A Commentary on Heidegger's "Being and Time," Division I*, 20.

21 William Blattner: "Dasein-with is not a distinct sort of being, but rather a more specific way in which Dasein can, indeed must, be. Heidegger writes, Dasein-with 'is neither occurrent [present-at-hand] nor available [ready-to-hand], but rather, is *just as* the Dasein itself who frees it'. (To 'free' Dasein-with means to let it show up for one)." Blattner, *Heidegger's Temporal Idealism*, 7 n. 2, emphasis in original.

22 Here is a helpful explanation of the distinction between the ontological and the ontic, from Hubert Dreyfus and Mark Wrathall: "A key element in Heidegger's argument is the distinction between the ontic and ontological. . . . Heidegger argues that traditional treatments of being have failed to adequately distinguish the two kinds of questions we can ask about being: the ontic question that asks about the properties of beings, and the ontological question that asks about ways or modes of being. Dasein, the available [aka, the ready-to-hand], and the occurrent [aka, the present-at-hand] are ontological categories. If one ontologically investigates an item of equipment, say, a pen, then one asks about the structures by virtue of which it is available or ready-to-hand. In an ontic inquiry, on the other hand, one asks about the properties, and the physical and relational structures peculiar to the pen." Hubert Dreyfus and Mark Wrathall, *Heidegger Reexamined. Volume 1: Dasein, Authenticity, and Death* (New York: Routledge, 2002), xiii.

23 Heidegger, *Being and Time*, 156–7, emphasis in original.

24 Heidegger, *Being and Time*, 158.

25 Blattner, *Heidegger's "Being and Time": A Reader's Guide*, 39. Blattner writes, "In pursuing my for-the-sakes-of-which I am engaging and sustaining the for-the-sakes-of-which of students and readers. Since the self-understanding of being a teacher is interwoven with the self-understanding of being a student, to act for the sake of being who I am is to act for the sake of others being who they are as well." Blattner, *Heidegger's "Being and Time": A Reader's Guide*, 67. Heidegger writes: "Thus as being-with, Dasein 'is' essentially for-the-sake-of others." Heidegger, *Being and Time*, 160, quoted in Blattner. As Stephen Mullhall writes, "[A]t least in part, Dasein establishes and maintains its relation to itself in and through its relations with Others." Stephen Mulhall, *Routledge Philosophy Guidebook to Heidegger and "Being and Time,"* (London: Routledge, 2005), 66.

26 Dreyfus, *Being-in-the-world: A Commentary on Heidegger's "Being and Time" Division I*, 148.

27 I am not claiming that it is impossible to become a budding philosopher without a seminar context. But my position does depend upon the claim that it is common for budding philosophers to rely upon seminar contexts for identity-work. And in those common cases, sociality is essential.

28 What about on-task smartphone-use? See Chapter 7.

29 Robert Rosenberger, drawing upon the work of the phenomenologist Aaron Gurwitsch, has made this point about technology generally, calling this phenomenon *field composition*: "With the notion of 'field composition', I refer to ways that some relations to technology involve substantial reorganizations of the total field of our awareness." Rosenberger, "The Phenomenological Case for Stricter Regulation of Cell Phones and Driving," 26.

30 We considered the high demands of maintaining engagement in a philosophy class in 2.4. The demands of continual engagement are similar regarding a small group of musicians making music together. In this case, for listeners and musicians, continuous listening will be essential to perceiving emerging aesthetic qualities, such as grooves and qualities of melodic and harmonic development (see Roholt, *Groove*). If our attention is only intermittent, we also miss something from other small-group situations. For example, a theme can emerge from a dinner conversation that we might miss when only intermittently paying attention. Sherry Turkle explains why the phrase—"Wait, what?"—is common for these reasons among smartphone-using college students. Cf. Turkle, *Reclaiming Conversation: The Power of Talk in a Digital Age*, 37.

31 There is much research demonstrating that the smartphone-use of others can be distracting to one. We encountered some of the research in 2.1. See the discussion there of Cho and Lee's study.

32 For an interesting discussion of related issues, see Turkle, *Reclaiming Conversation: The Power of Talk in a Digital Age*, 19–20.

33 Wolf allows for something like the degree of meaningfulness I am suggesting here: "the value of an activity or object in an individual life will vary depending on the relationship that the individual has to it and the role it plays in her life." Wolf, *Meaning in Life and Why It Matters*, 130.

34 Borgmann, *Technology and the Character of Contemporary Life*, 42.

35 Wolf, "The Meanings of Lives," 840.

36 Wolf, "The Meanings of Lives," 840.

37 Wolf, "The Meanings of Lives," 848 n. 4.

38 Blattner, *Heidegger's "Being and Time": A Reader's Guide*, 39.

7 A Note of Cautious Optimism

1 Recall that Borgmann does not use the word "paraphernalia"; he uses the word "instrument." I use "paraphernalia" partly in order to distinguish this category from musical instruments, which are focal things, and partly to mark a resonance with Heidegger's "equipment" [*Zeug*], as well as Don Ihde's concern with human-technology relations. *Calling-forth engagement* is a very general way in which such a piece of technology mediates our experience with focal practices.

2 Cf. Borgmann, *Technology and the Character of Contemporary Life*, 221.

3 Sherry Turkle describes a related problem: "If we think we might be interrupted, we keep conversations light, on topics of little controversy or consequence. And conversations with phones on the landscape block empathic connection. If two people are speaking and there is a phone on a nearby desk, each feels less connected to the other than when there is no phone present. Even a silent phone disconnects us." Turkle, *Reclaiming Conversation: The Power of Talk in a Digital Age*, 21. For the relevant research, see Turkle's notes.

4 I am thinking of Ihde's embodiment relation, hermeneutic relation, alterity relation, and so on. Cf. Don Ihde, *Technology and the Lifeworld: From*

Garden to Earth. Ihde's work kicked off the movement of the postphenomenology of technology; we brushed up against some of this work in Chapter 2. See Rosenberger and Verbeek (eds.), *Postphenomenological Investigations: Essays on Human-Technology Relations* (Lanham: Lexington Books, 2015). In addition to the work of Don Ihde, to see a philosophically insightful treatment of technological mediation, see the discussion of ultrasound in Peter-Paul Verbeek's *What Things Do* (University Park: The Pennsylvania State University Press, 2005). In an end note in which Borgmann discusses technological paraphernalia, he uses the term "mediate," but still under-emphasizes, in my view, the mediative impact of paraphernalia. Cf. Borgmann, *Technology and the Character of Contemporary Life*, 288 n.23.

5   Cf. Borgmann, *Technology and the Character of Contemporary Life*, 217. Writing philosophy or writing fiction are examples of activities that are worthwhile, in Wolf's sense (cf. Wolf, *Meaning in Life and Why It Matters*, 4).

6   Scrivener: https://www.literatureandlatte.com

7   Note that we are avoiding one area of potential smartphone-distraction in this example because such writing is not immediately social.

Bibliography

Alameddine, M., H. Soueidan, M. Makki, H. Tamim, and E. Hitti. "The Use of Smart Devices By Care Providers in Emergency Departments: Cross-Sectional Survey Design." *JMIR Mhealth Uhealth* 7, no. 6 (2019): e13614.

Alexander, Thomas M. *John Dewey's Theory of Art, Experience, and Nature.* Albany: State University of New York Press, 1987.

American College of Surgeons Committee on Perioperative Care. "Statement on Distractions in the Operating Room." *The Bulletin of the American College of Surgeons* 101, no. 10 (2016): 42–4.

Amez, Simon, and Stijn Baert. "Smartphone Use and Academic Performance: A Literature Review." *International Journal of Educational Research* 103 (2020): 7.

Association of periOperative Registered Nurses. "AORN Position Statement on Managing Distractions and Noise During Perioperative Patient Care." *AORN Journal* 111, no. 6 (2020): 675–80.

Bain, Ken. *What the Best College Teachers Do.* Cambridge, MA, and London: Harvard University Press, 2004.

Bernstein, Richard J. "John Dewey's Metaphysics of Experience." *Journal of Philosophy* LVIII, no. 1 (1961): 5–14.

Bernstein, Richard J. *John Dewey.* New York: Washington Square Press, 1966.

Blattner, William. *Heidegger's "Being and Time": A Reader's Guide.* London: Continuum, 2006.

Blattner, William. *Heidegger's Temporal Idealism.* Cambridge: Cambridge University Press, 1999.

Blattner, William. "Existence and Self-Understanding in Being and Time." In *Heidegger Reexamined*, Vol. 1: *Dasein, Authenticity, and Death*, edited by Hubert Dreyfus and Mark Wrathall, 177–90. New York: Routledge, 2002.

Borgmann, Albert. *Technology and the Character of Contemporary Life.* Chicago and London: University of Chicago Press, 1984.

Borgmann, Albert. *Crossing the Postmodern Divide.* Chicago: University of Chicago Press, 1992.

Borgmann, Albert. "Reply to My Critics." In *Technology and the Good Life?*, edited by Eric Higgs, Andrew Light, and David Strong. Chicago and London: University of Chicago Press, 2000.

Carman, Taylor. *Heidegger's Analytic: Interpretation, Discourse, and Authenticity*. Cambridge: Cambridge University Press, 2003.

Cheever, Nancy A., Larry D. Rosen, L. Mark Carrier, and Amber Chavez. "Out of Sight is Not Out of Mind: The Impact of Restricting Wireless Mobile Device Use on Anxiety Levels Among Low, Moderate and High Users." *Computers in Human Behavior* 37 (2014): 290–7.

Cho, Sumi, and Eunjoo Lee. "Distraction By Smartphone Use During Clinical Practice and Opinions About Smartphone Restriction Policies: A Cross-Sectional Descriptive Study of Nursing Students." *Nurse Education Today* 40 (2016): 128–33.

Dennett, Daniel C. "Information, Technology, and the Virtue of Ignorance." *Daedalus* 115 (1986): 135–53.

Dewey, John. *Logic: The Theory of Inquiry*. New York: Henry Holt and Company, 1938.

Dewey, John. *Art as Experience*. New York: Perigee, 1980 [1934].

Dewey, John. *Experience and Nature*. London: George Allen & Unwin Ltd, 1929.

Dreyfus, Hubert, and Sean D. Kelly. *All Things Shining: Reading the Western Classics to Find Meaning in a Secular Age*. New York: Free Press, 2011.

Dreyfus, Hubert. "Heidegger on Gaining a Free Relation to Technology." In *Heidegger Reexamined, Volume 3: Art, Poetry, and Technology*, edited by Hubert Dreyfus and Mark Wrathall. New York and London: Routledge, 2002.

Dreyfus, Hubert. *Being-in-the-world: A Commentary on Heidegger's "Being and Time," Division I*. Cambridge: MIT Press, 1991.

Dreyfus, Hubert. "Audio Lectures on Heidegger's Being and Time (Philosophy 185)" (2007).

Dreyfus, Hubert, and Mark Wrathall. *Heidegger Reexamined. Volume 1: Dasein, Authenticity, and Death*. New York: Routledge, 2002.

Dreyfus, Hubert, Charles Spinosa. "Highway Bridges and Feasts: Heidegger and Borgmann on How to Affirm Technology." In *Heidegger Reexamined. Volume 3: Art, Poetry, and Technology*, edited by Hubert Dreyfus and Mark Wrathall. New York and London: Routledge, 2002.

Feil, Michelle A. "Distractions in the Operating Room." In *Distracted Doctoring: Returning to Patient-Centered Care in the Digital Age*, edited by Stephen Bertman and Peter J. Papadakos. Berlin: Springer, 2017.

Feldman, Fred. *Pleasure and the Good Life*. Oxford and New York: Oxford University Press, 2004.

Fesmire, Steven. *Dewey*. London and New York: Routledge, 2015.

Finkel, Julia A, Daniel J. Kruger. "Is Cell Phone Use Socially Contagious?" *Human Ethology Bulletin* 27, no. 1–2 (2012): 15–17.

Fiorinelli, Massimo, Sofia Di Mario, Antonella Surace, Micol Mattei, Carla Russo, Giulia Villa, Sara Dionisi, Emanuele Di Simone, Noemi Giannetta, and Marco Di Muzio. "Smartphone Distraction During Nursing Care: Systematic Literature Review." *Applied Nursing Research* 58 (2021): 151405.

Fried, Carrie B. "In-Class Laptop Use and Its Effects on Student Learning." *Computers & Education* 50, no. 3 (2008): 906–14.

Garrett, Roland. "Dewey's Struggle With the Ineffable." *Transactions of the Charles S. Peirce Society* 9, no. 2 (1973): 95–109.

Gill, P., A. Kamath, and T. S. Gill. "Distraction: An Assessment of Smartphone Usage in Health Care Work Settings." *Risk Management and Healthcare Policy* 5 (2012): 105–14.

Halamka, John. "Order Interrupted by Text: Multitasking Mishap," *Patient Safety Network*. December 1, 2011. Available online at: https://psnet.ahrq.gov/web-mm/order-interrupted-text-multitasking-mishap

Haskins, Casey. "Dewey's Art as Experience in the Landscape of Twenty-First-century Aesthetics." In *The Oxford Handbook of Dewey*, edited by Steven Fesmire, 445–70. New York: Oxford University Press, 2019.

Haworth, Lawrence. "Focal Things and Focal Practices." In *Technology and the Good Life?*, edited by Eric Higgs, Andrew Light, and David Strong. Chicago and London: University of Chicago Press, 2000.

Heidegger, Martin. "On the Origin of the Work of Art." In *Poetry, Language, Thought*. New York: Harper & Row, 1971.

Heidegger, Martin. "The Thing." In *Poetry, Language, Thought*. New York: Harper & Row, 1971.

Heidegger, Martin. "The Question Concerning Technology." In *The Question Concerning Technology, and Other Essays*. Harper & Row, 1977.

Heidegger, Martin. *Being and Time*. Translated by John Macquarrie and Edward Robinson. Oxford: Blackwell Publishers Ltd, 1962 [1927].

Ihde, Don. *Technology and the Lifeworld: From Garden to Earth*. Bloomington and Indianapolis: Indiana University Press, 1990.

James, William. *The Principles of Psychology*. New York: Henry Holt & Co., 1890.

Jay, Martin. *Songs of Experience: Modern American and European Variations on a Universal Theme*. Berkeley and Los Angeles: University of California Press, 2005.

Jiang, Jingjing. "How Teens and Parents Navigate Screen Time and Device Distractions." *PEW Research Center* (August 22, 2018). Available online at: https://www.pewresearch.org/internet/2018/08/22/how-teens-and-parents-navigate-screen-time-and-device-distractions

Kennick, W. E. "Art and the Ineffable." *Journal of Philosophy* 58, no. 12 (1961): 309–20.

Kim, Inyeop, Rihun Kim, Heepyung Kim, Duyeon Kim, Kyungsik Han, Paul H. Lee, Gloria Mark, and Uichin Lee. "Understanding Smartphone Usage in College Classrooms: A Long-Term Measurement Study." *Computers & Education* 141 (2019): 103611.

Koch, Irwing, Hermann Müller, Edita Poljac, and Andrea Kiesel. "Cognitive Structure, Flexibility, and Plasticity in Human Multitasking—an Integrative Review of Dual-Task and Task-Switching Research." *Psychological Bulletin* 144, no. 6 (2018): 557–83.

Ma, Sihui, Daniel G. Steger, Peter E. Doolittle, Andrew H. Lee, Laura E. Griffin, and Amanda Stewart. "Persistence of Multitasking Distraction Following the Use of Smartphone-Based Clickers." *International Journal of Teaching and Learning in Higher Education* 32, no. 1 (2020): 64–72.

McBride, D., S. LeVasseur, and D. Li. "Nursing Performance and Mobile Phone Use: Are Nurses Aware of Their Performance Decrements?" *JMIR Hum Factors* 2, no. 1 (2015): e6.

Merleau-Ponty, Maurice. *Phenomenology of Perception*. Translated by Donald A. Landes. London and New York: Routledge, 2012 [1945].

Metz, Thaddeus. *Meaning in Life: An Analytic Study*. New York: Oxford University Press, 2013.

Michelfelder, Diane. "Driving While Beagleated." *Techné: Research in Philosophy and Technology* 18, no. 1–2 (2014): 117–32.

Mitchell, Andrew J., and Peter Trawny (eds.). *Heidegger's Black Notebooks: Responses to Anti-Semitism*. New York: Columbia University Press, 2017.

Mulhall, Stephen. *Routledge Philosophy Guidebook to Heidegger and "Being and Time."* London: Routledge, 2005.

Nietzsche, Friedrich. *The Gay Science*. Trans. Josefine Nauckhoff. Cambridge: Cambridge University Press, 2001.

Nozick, Robert. *Anarchy, State, and Utopia*. Oxford and Cambridge: Blackwell, 1974.

Nozick, Robert. *The Examined Life: Philosophical Meditations*. New York: Touchstone, 1989.

Pucciarelli, Gianluca, Silvio Simeone, Michele Virgolesi, Giuseppe Madonna, Maria Grazia Proietti, Gennaro Rocco, and Alessandro Stievano, "Nursing-Related Smartphone Activities in the Italian Nursing Population." *CIN: Computers, Informatics, Nursing* 37, no. 1 (2019): 29–38.

Richtel, Matt. "As Doctors Use More Devices, Potential for Distraction Grows." *New York Times*, December 14, 2011. Available online at: https://www.nytimes.com/2011/12/15/health/as-doctors-use-more-devices-potential-for-distraction-grows.html

Richtel, Matt. "Multitasking Doctor Imperils Patient, Case Study Says." *New York Times*, January 3, 2012. Available online at: https://bits.blogs.nytimes com/2012/01/03/multitasking-doctor-imperils-patient-case-study-says

Roholt, Tiger. "*Musical* Musical Nuance." *The Journal of Aesthetics and Art Criticism* 68, no. 1 (2010): 1–10.

Roholt, Tiger. *Groove: A Phenomenology of Rhythmic Nuance*. New York and London: Bloomsbury Academic, 2014.

Roholt, Tiger. "Being-with Smartphones," *Techné: Research in Philosophy and Technology* 25, no. 2 (2021): 284–307.

Roholt, Tiger. "Performance, Technology, and the Good Life." In *The Oxford Handbook of the Phenomenology of Music*, edited by Jonathan De Souza, Benjamin Steege, and Jessica Wiskus. Oxford: Oxford University Press, forthcoming.

Rosenberger, Robert. "The Phenomenological Case for Stricter Regulation of Cell Phones and Driving." *Techné: Research in Philosophy and Technology* (2014): 20–47.

Rosenberger, Robert, and Peter-Paul Verbeek. "A Postphenomenological Field Guide." In *Postphenomenological Investigations: Essays on Human-Technology Relations*, edited by Robert Rosenberger, Peter-Paul Verbeek. Lanham: Lexington Books, 2015.

Sahlström, Fritjof, Marie Tannerb, and Verneri Valasmo. "Connected Youth, Connected Classrooms. Smartphone Use and Student and Teacher Participation During Plenary Teaching." *Learning, Culture and Social Interaction* 21 (2019): 311–31.

Sana, Faria, Tina Weston, and Nicholas J. Cepeda. "Laptop Multitasking Hinders Classroom Learning for Both Users and Nearby Peers." *Computers & Education* 62 (2013): 24–31.

Sartre, Jean-Paul. "Existentialism is a Humanism." In *Existentialism: Basic Writings*, edited by Charles Guignon and Derk Pereboom, 290–308. Indianapolis: Hackett, 2001.

Schatzski, Theodore. "Being, the Clearing, and Realism." In *Heidegger Reexamined, Volume 2: Truth, Realism, and the History of Being*, edited by Hubert Dreyfus and Mark Wrathall, 177–94. New York: Routledge, 2002.

Schatzski, Theodore. "Early Heidegger on Sociality." In *A Companion to Heidegger*, edited by Hubert Dreyfus and Mark Wrathall, 233–47. Malden, MA: Blackwell Publishing, 2005.

Skaugset, L. Melissa, Susan Farrell, Michele Carney, Margaret Wolff, Sally A. Santen, Marcia Perry, and Stephen John Cico. "Can You Multitask? Evidence and Limitations of Task Switching and Multitasking in Emergency Medicine." *Annals of Emergency Medicine* 68, no. 2 (2016): 189–95.

Smith, T., E. Darling, and B. Searles. "2010 Survey on Cell Phone Use While
 Performing Cardiopulmonary Bypass." *Perfusion* 26, no. 5 (2011): 375–80.
Srivastava, L. "Mobile Phones and the Evolution of Social Behaviour." *Behaviour
 & Information Technology* 24, no. 2 (2005): 111–29.
Strong, David. *Crazy Mountains*. Albany: State University of New York Press, 1995.
Strong, David. "Philosophy in the Service of Things." In *Technology and the Good
 Life?*, edited by Eric Higgs, Andrew Light, and David Strong, 316–38.
 Chicago: The University of Chicago Press, 2000.
Strong, David, and Eric Higgs. "Borgmann's Philosophy of Technology." In
 Technology and the Good Life?, edited by Eric Higgs, Andrew Light, and
 David Strong. Chicago and London: University of Chicago Press, 2000.
Stuhr, John J. "Dewey's Notion of Qualitative Experience." *Transactions of the
 Charles S. Peirce Society* 15, no. 1 (1979): 68–82.
Sturt, George. *The Wheelwright's Shop*. Cambridge: Cambridge University Press,
 1923.
Taylor, Charles. *Sources of the Self: The Making of the Modern Identity*.
 Cambridge: Harvard University Press, 1989.
Tombu, Michael N., Christopher L. Asplund, Paul E. Dux, Douglass Godwin,
 Justin W. Martin, and René Marois. "A Unified Attentional Bottleneck in the
 Human Brain." *PNAS* 108, no. 33 (2011): 13426–31.
Turkle, Sherry. *Reclaiming Conversation: The Power of Talk in a Digital Age*. New
 York: Penguin, 2015.
Verbeek, Peter-Paul. *What Things Do*. University Park: The Pennsylvania State
 University Press, 2005.
Vincent, Jane. *Emotion in the Social Practices of Mobile Phone Users*. Guildford:
 University of Surrey 2011. Available online at: https://ethos.bl.uk/
 OrderDetails.do?uin=uk.bl.ethos.543914
Vincent, Jane. "Emotional Attachment and Mobile Phones." *Knowledge
 Technology and Policy* 19, no. 1 (2006), 39–44.
Vincent, Jane. "Emotion and Mobile Phones." In *Mobile Democracy:
 Communications in the 21st Century*. Edited by Kristóf Nyíri. Vienna:
 Passagen Verlag, 2003.
Wellner, Galit. "Multi-Attention and the Horcrux Logic: Justifications for Talking
 on the Cell Phone While Driving." *Techné: Research in Philosophy and
 Technology* 18, no. 1–2 (2014): 48–73.
Wittgenstein, Ludwig. *The Blue and Brown Books*. Oxford: Blackwell, 1998
 [1933–1935].
Wolf, Susan. "The Meanings of Lives." In *Introduction to Philosophy: Classical
 and Contemporary Readings*, edited by John Perry, Michael Bratman, and
 John Martin Fischer. New York: Oxford University Press, 2016 [originally
 2007].

Wolf, Susan. *Meaning in Life and Why It Matters.* Princeton University Press, 2010.
Wolf, Susan. "Meaning in Life: Meeting the Challenges." *Foundations of Science* 21, no. 2 (2014): 279–82.
Wolf, Susan. "Meaningfulness: A Third Dimension of the Good Life." *Foundations of Science* 21, no. 2 (2014): 253–69.

Index